WILLIAM SHAKESPEARE
OTHELLO

Illustrated by Oscar Zarate

OVAL PROJECTS LIMITED
SIDGWICK & JACKSON LIMITED

Published by Oval Projects Limited
335 Kennington Road, London SE11 4QE

British Library Cataloguing in Publication Data
Shakespeare, William
    Othello.
    1. Shakespeare, William. Othello–Pictorial works
    I. Title   II. Zarate, Oscar
    822.3'3   PR2829

ISBN 0 283 99024 4 hardcover
ISBN 0 283 99025 2 softcover

Edited by David Gibson & Anne Tauté
Series design by Jim Wire, Charing, Kent
Lettering by Elitta Fell, Westerham, Kent

Front cover illustration designed, assembled
and retouched by Jim Wire

Origination by Adroit Photo Litho Limited, Birmingham
Printed by Mandarin Offset (HK) Limited, Hong Kong
Distributed by Sidgwick & Jackson Limited, London

A special package of this book and two audiocassette recordings
of the BBC World Drama Production of Othello, starring Paul
Scofield, Nicol Williamson and Rosalind Shanks, is available from
BBC External Business and Development Group, Bush House,
London WC2.

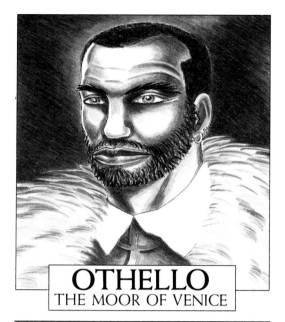

OTHELLO
THE MOOR OF VENICE

DESDEMONA
WIFE TO OTHELLO

IAGO
A VILLAIN

CASSIO
AN HONOURABLE LIEUTENANT

EMILIA
WIFE TO IAGO

RODERIGO
A GULLED GENTLEMAN

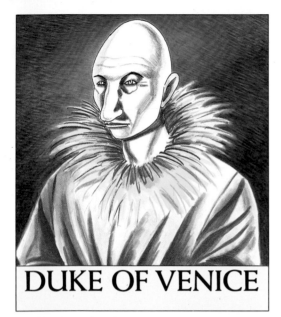

DUKE OF VENICE

BRABANTIO
FATHER TO DESDEMONA

MONTANO
GOVERNOR OF CYPRUS

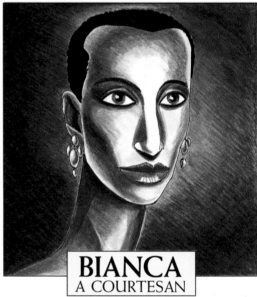

BIANCA
A COURTESAN

LODOVICO   GRATIANO
TWO NOBLE VENETIANS

THE STORY

Othello, a black general in the Venetian army, has promoted **Cassio** as his Lieutenant, over the head of **Iago,** a more experienced soldier. Iago, full of anger and resentment, seeks revenge.

Othello has secretly married **Desdemona,** daughter of a wealthy Senator. Iago conspires with **Roderigo,** one of Desdemona's rejected admirers. They rudely inform Desdemona's father that his daughter has run away with the Moor. Othello is summoned before the Senate. He convinces the **Duke of Venice** that Desdemona has not married him against her will.

News comes of war, and Othello is instructed to sail for Cyprus, a Venetian possession, to command its defence against the Turks.

All arrive in Cyprus to find that a storm has destroyed the enemy's fleet. During the celebrations Iago makes Cassio drunk. Othello strips Cassio of his office, but at Iago's suggestion, Cassio asks Desdemona to plead for his reinstatement with Othello. This she does, so warmly, that Iago by subtle hints and innuendo leads Othello to believe that Desdemona and Cassio are lovers.

Desdemona's handkerchief is given to Iago by his wife, **Emilia.** Iago plants it on Cassio and tells Othello he has seen Cassio with it. Iago contrives a meeting with Cassio and hides Othello nearby. Cassio talks of his mistress, **Bianca,** but Othello thinks he is speaking of Desdemona. Convinced of her infidelity Othello vows her death.

Iago offers on Othello's behalf to murder Cassio, but persuades Roderigo to do it for him. In the dark Roderigo misses Cassio but is himself wounded. Iago then wounds Cassio, and fearful of disclosure, stabs Roderigo. Othello overhears Roderigo's wretched cry and believes it to be Cassio's confession. Now certain of Desdemona's guilt, Othello smothers her.

Emilia discovers the murder and exposes Iago's treachery. Iago knifes her and is caught trying to escape. All is revealed.

Overwhelmed by grief and remorse, Othello kills himself.

THE TRAGEDY OF OTHELLO, MOOR OF VENICE

To theatregoing Londoners in the early 1600's, Italy meant crime rather than art, the devious head rather than the simple heart. Venice suggested both the riches that breed intrigue, and the manners that love to hide the face behind a mask. The simple heart demanded that men and women should be what they seem: the beautiful should be good, the deformed should be perverted, the black-skinned should be black-hearted. Accordingly, literature and theatre were terribly fascinated by the fact that people could be, inside, so unlike what they seemed. And it was even more perplexing that this problem was greatest in the most civilized surroundings. It is a cheating world in which Othello appears, bearing an innocent nobility of soul, and bearing it, perplexingly, behind a black 'mask.'

Elizabethans saw anyone dark-skinned, from south of the Mediterranean, as a 'Moor,' and Othello is one of the darkest – a 'blackamoor.' The King of Morocco's ambassador – a 'tawny Moor' – had visited London in 1600, and that there were "great numbers of Negars and Black-a-Moors" in London is clear from Elizabeth I's edicts, in 1599 and 1601, commanding them to be "discharged out of this Her Majesty's dominions." Interest in fabulous Africa was running high with the publication, in 1600, of A Geographical History of Africa by Leo Africanus. With the first recorded performance of Othello in 1604 – though it may have received its première earlier, and been in the writing since 1601 – it may be that the time was ripe for a dramatist to look into the soul beneath the black skin. Certainly the racist convention (earlier followed by Shakespeare himself) that peddled black characters as easy stage villains or mindless exotics, was ended by Othello.

The Moor is not long in Venice, however, for the site of his tragedy is to be Cyprus. Again there are ironies: Cyprus was the isle of love, the 'Cythera' where legend placed the birth of Venus, Love's goddess. And Othello goes to be its governor, to defend it from the barbarous Turks: when Othello was written, Cyprus had already fallen to the Turks, in 1570, amid scenes of notorious atrocity.

The tragedy is one of doomed love: the honest heart cannot withstand the terrible suspicion of cheating. Jealousy, envy and resentment pervade the play. Brabantio is the jealous father, Roderigo the jealous suitor, Bianca the jealous mistress; Cassio is 'jealous of his reputation,' Emilia is jealous of the power of men. Even Desdemona 'wished that Heaven had made her such a man.' Even the clown exhibits the truculence of the powerless. But no one in the play is more jealous than Iago: beneath that plausible exterior lies a swamp of sexual, professional and class jealousy, a Satanic urge to adulterate and spoil everyone and every value above and beyond itself. Add racial hatred, and the pattern is clear: Iago simply transfuses his disease into Othello's blood. And he does it by playing on similar insecurities in his victim, for Othello only succumbs when – for the first time it seems – he is made to think about his age, his blackness, his lack of civilized manners, his ignorance of the 'super-subtle' world – and that Desdemona, his love, his wife, has, herself, deceived; has, herself, seemed to be what she was not. 'Chaos is come again': the simple heart is suddenly lost in a terrifying maze of uncertainty, and the only outlet can only be an act of terrible certainty – an act such as, on battle fields, has filled his life with certainty – to kill.

Finally, consider the clown. He puns. That appalled fascination with dishonesty that makes the play obsessively repeat 'Honest Iago' while knowing he has said 'I am not what I am,' becomes at the comic level an obsession with puns, 'double meanings,' where 'nothing is but what is not.' The mask – the very symbol of the theatre – has become, itself, 'the torture of the mind.' The world's turned upside down: the lovers come to Cyprus to die.

David Gibson

1

BUT HE, AS LOVING HIS OWN PRIDE AND PURPOSES, EVADES THEM WITH A BOMBAST CIRCUMSTANCE HORRIBLY STUFFED WITH EPITHETS OF WAR,

NONSUITS MY MEDIATORS: FOR "CERTES" SAYS HE, "I HAVE ALREADY CHOSE MY OFFICER."

AND WHAT WAS HE?

FORSOOTH, A GREAT ARITHMETICIAN, ONE MICHAEL CASSIO, A FLORENTINE, —A FELLOW ALMOST DAMNED IN A FAIR WIFE — THAT NEVER SET A SQUADRON IN THE FIELD,

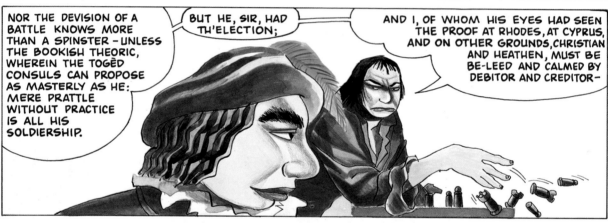

NOR THE DEVISION OF A BATTLE KNOWS MORE THAN A SPINSTER — UNLESS THE BOOKISH THEORIC, WHEREIN THE TOGÈD CONSULS CAN PROPOSE AS MASTERLY AS HE: MERE PRATTLE WITHOUT PRACTICE IS ALL HIS SOLDIERSHIP.

BUT HE, SIR, HAD TH'ELECTION;

AND I, OF WHOM HIS EYES HAD SEEN THE PROOF AT RHODES, AT CYPRUS, AND ON OTHER GROUNDS, CHRISTIAN AND HEATHEN, MUST BE BE-LEED AND CALMED BY DEBITOR AND CREDITOR—

THIS COUNTER-CASTER, HE IN GOOD TIME MUST HIS LIEUTENANT BE, AND I — GOD BLESS THE MARK!— HIS MOORSHIP'S ANCIENT.

BY HEAVEN, I RATHER WOULD HAVE BEEN HIS HANGMAN.

WHY, THERE'S NO REMEDY. 'TIS THE CURSE OF SERVICE: PREFERMENT GOES BY LETTER AND AFFECTION, AND NOT BY OLD GRADATION, WHERE EACH SECOND STOOD HEIR TO THE FIRST.

NOW, SIR, BE JUDGE YOURSELF WHETHER I IN ANY JUST TERM AM AFFINED TO LOVE THE MOOR.

I WOULD NOT FOLLOW HIM THEN.

O, SIR, CONTENT YOU: I FOLLOW HIM TO SERVE MY TURN UPON HIM.

WE CANNOT ALL BE MASTERS, NOR ALL MASTERS CANNOT BE TRULY FOLLOWED.

WHAT A FULL FORTUNE DOES THE THICK-LIPS OWE IF HE CAN CARRY'T THUS!

CALL UP HER FATHER: ROUSE HIM, MAKE AFTER HIM, POISON HIS DELIGHT, PROCLAIM HIM IN THE STREETS. INCENSE HER KINSMEN, AND THOUGH HE IN A FERTILE CLIMATE DWELL, PLAGUE HIM WITH FLIES: THOUGH THAT HIS JOY BE JOY, YET THROW SUCH CHANCES OF VEXATION ON'T AS IT MAY LOSE SOME COLOUR.

HERE IS HER FATHER'S HOUSE: I'LL CALL ALOUD.

DO, WITH LIKE TIMOROUS ACCENT AND DIRE YELL, AS WHEN, BY NIGHT AND NEGLIGENCE, THE FIRE IS SPIED IN POPULOUS CITIES.

WHAT HO! BRABANTIO! SIGNOR BRABANTIO, HO!

AWAKE! WHAT HO, BRABANTIO! THIEVES, THIEVES! LOOK TO YOUR HOUSE, YOUR DAUGHTER AND YOUR BAGS! THIEVES, THIEVES!

WHAT IS THE REASON OF THIS TERRIBLE SUMMONS? WHAT IS THE MATTER THERE?

SIGNOR, IS ALL YOUR FAMILY WITHIN?

ARE YOUR DOORS LOCKED?

WHY? WHEREFORE ASK YOU THIS?

ZOUNDS, SIR, YOU'RE ROBBED, FOR SHAME, PUT ON YOUR GOWN, YOUR HEART IS BURST, YOU HAVE LOST HALF YOUR SOUL! EVEN NOW, NOW, VERY NOW, AN OLD BLACK RAM IS TUPPING YOUR WHITE EWE.

ARISE, ARISE, AWAKE THE SNORTING CITIZENS WITH THE BELL, OR ELSE THE DEVIL WILL MAKE A GRANDSIRE OF YOU. ARISE I SAY!

WHAT! HAVE YOU LOST YOUR WITS?

MOST REVEREND SIGNOR, DO YOU KNOW MY VOICE?

NOT I: WHAT ARE YOU?

MY NAME IS RODERIGO.

THE WORSER WELCOME: I HAVE CHARGED THEE NOT TO HAUNT ABOUT MY DOORS; IN HONEST PLAINNESS THOU HAST HEARD ME SAY MY DAUGHTER IS NOT FOR THEE.

AND NOW, IN MADNESS, BEING FULL OF SUPPER AND DISTEMPERING DRAUGHTS, UPON MALICIOUS BRAVERY DOST THOU COME TO START MY QUIET.

SIR, SIR, SIR—

BUT THOU MUST NEEDS BE SURE MY SPIRITS AND MY PLACE HAVE IN THEM POWER TO MAKE THIS BITTER TO THEE.

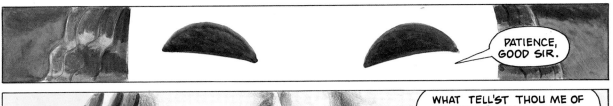

PATIENCE, GOOD SIR.

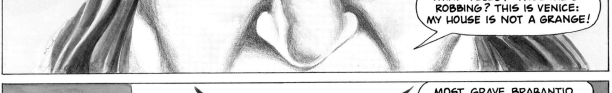

WHAT TELL'ST THOU ME OF ROBBING? THIS IS VENICE: MY HOUSE IS NOT A GRANGE!

MOST GRAVE BRABANTIO, IN SIMPLE AND PURE SOUL I COME TO YOU—

ZOUNDS, SIR, YOU ARE ONE OF THOSE THAT WILL NOT SERVE GOD IF THE DEVIL BID YOU. BECAUSE WE HAVE COME TO DO YOU SERVICE, AND YOU THINK WE ARE RUFFIANS, YOU'LL HAVE YOUR DAUGHTER COVERED WITH A BARBARY HORSE, YOU'LL HAVE YOUR NEPHEWS NEIGH TO YOU, YOU'LL HAVE COURSERS FOR COUSINS, AND JENNETS FOR GERMANS.

WHAT PROFANE WRETCH ART THOU?

I AM ONE, SIR, THAT COMES TO TELL YOU YOUR DAUGHTER AND THE MOOR ARE NOW MAKING THE BEAST WITH TWO BACKS.

THOU ART A VILLAIN!

YOU ARE A SENATOR.

THIS THOU SHALT ANSWER.

I KNOW THEE, RODERIGO.

SIR, I WILL ANSWER ANYTHING. BUT I BESEECH YOU IF'T BE YOUR PLEASURE AND MOST WISE CONSENT (AS PARTLY I FIND IT IS) THAT YOUR FAIR DAUGHTER, AT THIS ODD-EVEN AND DULL WATCH O'TH'NIGHT, TRANSPORTED WITH NO WORSE NOR BETTER GUARD, BUT WITH A KNAVE OF COMMON HIRE, A GONDOLIER, TO THE GROSS CLASPS OF A LASCIVIOUS MOOR—

IF THIS BE KNOWN TO YOU, AND YOUR ALLOWANCE, WE THEN HAVE DONE YOU BOLD AND SAUCY WRONGS. BUT IF YOU KNOW NOT THIS, MY MANNERS TELL ME WE HAVE YOUR WRONG REBUKE.

DO NOT BELIEVE THAT FROM THE SENSE OF ALL CIVILITY I THUS WOULD PLAY AND TRIFLE WITH YOUR REVERENCE. YOUR DAUGHTER, IF YOU HAVE NOT GIVEN HER LEAVE, I SAY AGAIN HATH MADE A GROSS REVOLT, TYING HER DUTY, BEAUTY, WIT, AND FORTUNES IN AN EXTRAVAGANT AND WHEELING STRANGER OF HERE AND EVERYWHERE.

STRAIGHT SATISFY YOURSELF: IF SHE BE IN HER CHAMBER, OR YOUR HOUSE, LET LOOSE ON ME THE JUSTICE OF THE STATE FOR THUS DELUDING YOU.

STRIKE ON THE TINDER, HO! GIVE ME A TAPER! CALL UP ALL MY PEOPLE! —THIS ACCIDENT IS NOT UNLIKE MY DREAM: BELIEF OF IT OPPRESSES ME ALREADY.

LIGHT I SAY, LIGHT!

FAREWELL, FOR I MUST LEAVE YOU. IT SEEMS NOT MEET NOR WHOLESOME TO MY PLACE TO BE PRODUCED—AS IF I STAY, I SHALL—AGAINST THE MOOR.

FOR I DO KNOW THE STATE, HOWEVER THIS MAY GALL HIM WITH SOME CHECK, CANNOT WITH SAFETY CAST HIM;

FOR HE'S EMBARKED WITH SUCH LOUD REASON TO THE CYPRUS WARS, WHICH EVEN NOW STAND IN ACT, THAT FOR THEIR SOULS ANOTHER OF HIS FATHOM THEY HAVE NONE TO LEAD THEIR BUSINESS.

IN WHICH REGARD, THOUGH I DO HATE HIM AS I DO HELL PAINS, YET FOR NECESSITY OF PRESENT LIFE I MUST SHOW OUT A FLAG AND SIGN OF LOVE— WHICH IS INDEED BUT SIGN.

THAT YOU SHALL SURELY FIND HIM, LEAD TO THE SAGITTARY THE RAISÈD SEARCH; AND THERE WILL I BE WITH HIM.

SO FAREWELL.

IT IS TOO TRUE AN EVIL. GONE SHE IS, AND WHAT'S TO COME OF MY DESPISÈD TIME IS NAUGHT BUT BITTERNESS.

NOW, RODERIGO, WHERE DIDST THOU SEE HER?— O UNHAPPY GIRL!— WITH THE MOOR, SAYEST THOU?— WHO WOULD BE A FATHER?— HOW DIDST THOU KNOW 'TWAS SHE?

—O SHE DECEIVES ME PAST THOUGHT!— WHAT SAID SHE TO YOU?

—GET MORE TAPERS! RAISE ALL MY KINDRED!

—ARE THEY MARRIED THINK YOU?

TRULY I THINK THEY ARE.

O HEAVEN, HOW GOT SHE OUT? O TREASON OF THE BLOOD! FATHERS, FROM HENCE TRUST NOT YOUR DAUGHTERS' MINDS BY WHAT YOU SEE THEM ACT. IS THERE NOT CHARMS BY WHICH THE PROPERTY OF YOUTH AND MAIDHOOD MAY BE ABUSED?

HAVE YOU NOT READ, RODERIGO, OF SOME SUCH THING?

YES, SIR, I HAVE INDEED.

CALL UP MY BROTHER!—O WOULD YOU HAD HAD HER—SOME ONE WAY, SOME ANOTHER!—DO YOU KNOW WHERE WE MAY APPREHEND HER AND THE MOOR?

I THINK I CAN DISCOVER HIM, IF YOU PLEASE TO GET GOOD GUARD AND GO ALONG WITH ME.

PRAY YOU LEAD ON. AT EVERY HOUSE I'LL CALL— I MAY COMMAND AT MOST.

GET WEAPONS, HO!—

AND RAISE SOME SPECIAL OFFICERS OF NIGHT.

ON, GOOD RODERIGO. I'LL DESERVE YOUR PAINS.

7

BUT LOOK, WHAT LIGHTS COME YOND?

ENTER CASSIO

THOSE ARE THE RAISÈD FATHER AND HIS FRIENDS: YOU WERE BEST GO IN.

NOT I: I MUST BE FOUND. MY PARTS, MY TITLE, AND MY PERFECT SOUL SHALL MANIFEST ME RIGHTLY.

IS IT THEY?

BY JANUS, I THINK NO.

THE SERVANTS OF THE DUKE—AND MY LIEUTENANT!

THE GOODNESS OF THE NIGHT UPON YOU, FRIENDS. WHAT IS THE NEWS?

THE DUKE DOES GREET YOU, GENERAL, AND HE REQUIRES YOUR HASTE-POST-HASTE APPEARANCE EVEN ON THE INSTANT.

WHAT IS THE MATTER, THINK YOU?

SOMETHING FROM CYPRUS, AS I MAY DIVINE: IT IS A BUSINESS OF SOME HEAT.

THE GALLEYS HAVE SENT A DOZEN SEQUENT MESSENGERS THIS VERY NIGHT AT ONE ANOTHER'S HEELS; AND MANY OF THE CONSULS, RAISED AND MET, ARE AT THE DUKE'S ALREADY. YOU HAVE BEEN HOTLY CALLED FOR, WHEN, BEING NOT AT YOUR LODGING TO BE FOUND, THE SENATE SENT ABOUT THREE SEVERAL QUESTS TO SEARCH YOU OUT.

'TIS WELL I AM FOUND BY YOU: I WILL BUT SPEND A WORD HERE IN THE HOUSE AND GO WITH YOU.

ANCIENT, WHAT MAKES HE HERE?

FAITH, HE TONIGHT HATH BOARDÈD A LAND CARACK: IF IT PROVE LAWFUL PRIZE, HE'S MADE FOR EVER.

I DO NOT UNDERSTAND.

HE'S MARRIED.

TO WHO?

MARRY, TO—

COME, CAPTAIN, WILL YOU GO?

HAVE WITH YOU.

THERE IS NO COMPOSITION IN THESE NEWS THAT GIVES THEM CREDIT.

INDEED THEY ARE DISPROPORTIONED: MY LETTERS SAY A HUNDRED AND SEVEN GALLEYS.

AND MINE A HUNDRED AND FORTY.

AND MINE TWO HUNDRED; BUT THOUGH THEY JUMP NOT ON A JUST ACCOMPT—

AS IN THESE CASES, WHERE THEY AIM REPORTS 'TIS OFT WITH DIFFERENCE— YET DO THEY ALL CONFIRM A TURKISH FLEET, AND BEARING UP TO CYPRUS.

WHAT HO! WHAT HO! WHAT HO!

A MESSENGER FROM THE GALLEYS.

NAY, IT IS POSSIBLE ENOUGH TO JUDGEMENT: I DO NOT SO SECURE ME IN THE ERROR, BUT THE MAIN ARTICLE I DO APPROVE IN FEARFUL SENSE.

NOW WHAT'S THE BUSINESS?

THE TURKISH PREPARATION MAKES FOR RHODES; SO WAS I BID REPORT HERE TO THE STATE BY SIGNOR ANGELO.

HOW SAY YOU BY THIS CHANGE?

THIS CANNOT BE, BY NO ASSAY OF REASON. 'TIS A PAGEANT TO KEEP US IN FALSE GAZE— WHEN WE CONSIDER TH'IMPORTANCY OF CYPRUS TO THE TURK... AND LET OURSELVES AGAIN BUT UNDERSTAND THAT AS IT MORE CONCERNS THE TURK THAN RHODES, SO MAY HE WITH MORE FACILE QUESTION BEAR IT, FOR THAT IT STANDS NOT IN SUCH WARLIKE BRACE, BUT ALTOGETHER LACKS TH'ABILITIES THAT RHODES IS DRESSED IN.

IF WE MAKE THOUGHT OF THIS, WE MUST NOT THINK THE TURK IS SO UNSKILFUL TO LEAVE THAT LATEST WHICH CONCERNS HIM FIRST, NEGLECTING AN ATTEMPT OF EASE AND GAIN TO WAKE AND WAGE A DANGER PROFITLESS.

NAY, IN ALL CONFIDENCE HE'S NOT FOR RHODES.

HERE IS MORE NEWS.

ENTER MESSENGER

THE OTTOMITES, REVEREND AND GRACIOUS, STEERING WITH DUE COURSE TOWARD THE ISLE OF RHODES, HAVE THERE INJOINTED WITH AN AFTER FLEET.

AY, SO I THOUGHT. HOW MANY, AS YOU GUESS?

OF THIRTY SAIL; AND NOW THEY DO RE-STEM THEIR BACKWARD COURSE, BEARING WITH FRANK APPEARANCE THEIR PURPOSES TOWARD CYPRUS. SIGNOR MONTANO, YOUR TRUSTY AND MOST VALIANT SERVITOR, WITH HIS FREE DUTY RECOMMENDS YOU THUS, AND PRAYS YOU TO BELIEVE HIM.

'TIS CERTAIN THEN FOR CYPRUS. MARCUS LUCCICOS, IS NOT HE IN TOWN?

HE'S NOW IN FLORENCE.

WRITE FROM US: WISH HIM POST-POST-HASTE DISPATCH.

HERE COMES BRABANTIO, AND THE VALIANT MOOR.

VALIANT OTHELLO, WE MUST STRAIGHT EMPLOY YOU AGAINST THE GENERAL ENEMY OTTOMAN.

I DID NOT SEE YOU: WELCOME, GENTLE SIGNOR; WE LACKED YOUR COUNSEL AND YOUR HELP TONIGHT.

SO DID I YOURS. GOOD YOUR GRACE, PARDON ME:

NEITHER MY PLACE, NOR AUGHT I HEARD OF BUSINESS, HATH RAISED ME FROM MY BED; NOR DOTH THE GENERAL CARE TAKE HOLD ON ME, FOR MY PARTICULAR GRIEF IS OF SO FLOOD-GATE AND O'ERBEARING NATURE THAT IT ENGLUTS AND SWALLOWS OTHER SORROWS AND YET IS STILL ITSELF.

WHY? WHAT'S THE MATTER?

MY DAUGHTER! O, MY DAUGHTER!

DEAD?

AY, TO ME. SHE IS ABUSED, STOLEN FROM ME, AND CORRUPTED BY SPELLS AND MEDICINES BOUGHT OF MOUNTEBANKS; FOR NATURE SO PREPOSTEROUSLY TO ERR, BEING NOT DEFICIENT, BLIND, OR LAME OF SENSE, SANS WITCHCRAFT COULD NOT.

WHOE'ER HE BE THAT IN THIS FOUL PROCEEDING HATH THUS BEGUILED YOUR DAUGHTER OF HERSELF, AND YOU OF HER, THE BLOODY BOOK OF LAW YOU SHALL YOURSELF READ, IN THE BITTER LETTER, AFTER YOUR OWN SENSE —YEA, THOUGH OUR PROPER SON STOOD IN YOUR ACTION.

HUMBLY I THANK YOUR GRACE. HERE IS THE MAN: THIS MOOR, WHOM NOW IT SEEMS YOUR SPECIAL MANDATE FOR THE STATE AFFAIRS HATH HITHER BROUGHT.

WE ARE VERY SORRY FOR'T.

WHAT IN YOUR OWN PART CAN YOU SAY TO THIS?

NOTHING, BUT THIS IS SO.

MOST POTENT, GRAVE AND REVEREND SIGNORS, MY VERY NOBLE AND APPROVED GOOD MASTERS; THAT I HAVE TA'EN AWAY THIS OLD MAN'S DAUGHTER, IT IS MOST TRUE; TRUE I HAVE MARRIED HER— THE VERY HEAD AND FRONT OF MY OFFENDING HATH THIS EXTENT, NO MORE.

RUDE AM I IN MY SPEECH, AND LITTLE BLESSED WITH THE SOFT PHRASE OF PEACE; FOR SINCE THESE ARMS OF MINE HAD SEVEN YEARS' PITH TILL NOW, SOME NINE MOONS WASTED, THEY HAVE USED THEIR DEAREST ACTION IN THE TENTED FIELD.

AND LITTLE OF THIS GREAT WORLD CAN I SPEAK MORE THAN PERTAINS TO FEATS OF BROIL AND BATTLE: AND THEREFORE LITTLE SHALL I GRACE MY CAUSE IN SPEAKING FOR MYSELF.

YET, BY YOUR GRACIOUS PATIENCE, I WILL A ROUND UNVARNISHED TALE DELIVER OF MY WHOLE COURSE OF LOVE: WHAT DRUGS, WHAT CHARMS, WHAT CONJURATION AND WHAT MIGHTY MAGIC—FOR SUCH PROCEEDINGS AM I CHARGED WITHAL— I WON HIS DAUGHTER.

A MAIDEN NEVER BOLD; OF SPIRIT SO STILL AND QUIET THAT HER MOTION BLUSHED AT HER SELF: AND SHE, IN SPITE OF NATURE, OF YEARS, OF COUNTRY, CREDIT, EVERYTHING, TO FALL IN LOVE WITH WHAT SHE FEARED TO LOOK ON?

IT IS A JUDGEMENT MAIMED AND MOST IMPERFECT THAT WILL CONFESS PERFECTION SO COULD ERR AGAINST ALL RULES OF NATURE—AND MUST BE DRIVEN TO FIND OUT PRACTICES OF CUNNING HELL WHY THIS SHOULD BE.

I THEREFORE VOUCH AGAIN THAT WITH SOME MIXTURES POWERFUL O'ER THE BLOOD, OR WITH SOME DRAM CONJURED TO THIS EFFECT, HE WROUGHT UPON HER.

TO VOUCH THIS IS NO PROOF, WITHOUT MORE WIDER AND MORE OVERT TEST THAN THESE THIN HABITS AND POOR LIKELIHOODS OF MODERN SEEMING DO PREFER AGAINST HIM.

BUT OTHELLO SPEAK:

DID YOU BY INDIRECT AND FORCÈD COURSES SUBDUE AND POISON THIS YOUNG MAID'S AFFECTIONS? OR CAME IT BY REQUEST AND SUCH FAIR QUESTION AS SOUL TO SOUL AFFORDETH?

I DO BESEECH YOU, SEND FOR THE LADY TO THE SAGITTARY, AND LET HER SPEAK OF ME BEFORE HER FATHER. IF YOU DO FIND ME FOUL IN HER REPORT, THE TRUST, THE OFFICE I DO HOLD OF YOU, NOT ONLY TAKE AWAY, BUT LET YOUR SENTENCE EVEN FALL UPON MY LIFE.

FETCH DESDEMONA HITHER.

ANCIENT, CONDUCT THEM: YOU BEST KNOW THE PLACE.

AND TILL SHE COME, AS TRULY AS TO HEAVEN I DO CONFESS THE VICES OF MY BLOOD, SO JUSTLY TO YOUR GRAVE EARS I'LL PRESENT HOW I DID THRIVE IN THIS FAIR LADY'S LOVE, AND SHE IN MINE.

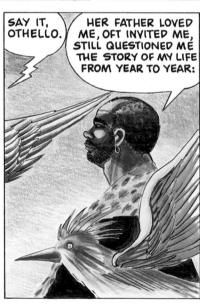

SAY IT, OTHELLO.

HER FATHER LOVED ME, OFT INVITED ME, STILL QUESTIONED ME THE STORY OF MY LIFE FROM YEAR TO YEAR:

THE BATTLES, SIEGES, FORTUNES THAT I HAVE PASSED. I RAN IT THROUGH EVEN FROM MY BOYISH DAYS TO THE VERY MOMENT THAT HE BADE ME TELL IT.

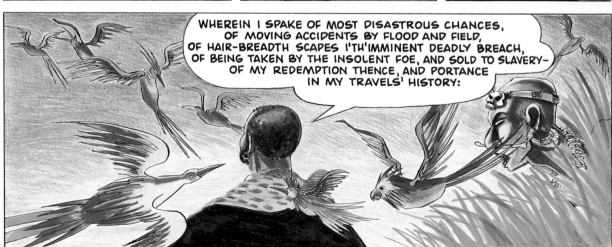

WHEREIN I SPAKE OF MOST DISASTROUS CHANCES, OF MOVING ACCIDENTS BY FLOOD AND FIELD, OF HAIR-BREADTH SCAPES I'TH'IMMINENT DEADLY BREACH, OF BEING TAKEN BY THE INSOLENT FOE, AND SOLD TO SLAVERY— OF MY REDEMPTION THENCE, AND PORTANCE IN MY TRAVELS' HISTORY:

16

MY STORY BEING DONE, SHE GAVE ME FOR MY PAINS A WORLD OF SIGHS: SHE SWORE, IN FAITH 'TWAS STRANGE, 'TWAS PASSING STRANGE, 'TWAS PITIFUL, 'TWAS WONDROUS PITIFUL;

SHE WISHED SHE HAD NOT HEARD IT, YET SHE WISHED THAT HEAVEN HAD MADE HER SUCH A MAN. SHE THANKED ME, AND BADE ME, IF I HAD A FRIEND THAT LOVED HER,

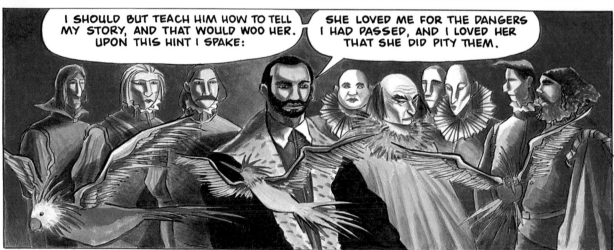

I SHOULD BUT TEACH HIM HOW TO TELL MY STORY, AND THAT WOULD WOO HER. UPON THIS HINT I SPAKE:

SHE LOVED ME FOR THE DANGERS I HAD PASSED, AND I LOVED HER THAT SHE DID PITY THEM.

THIS ONLY IS THE WITCHCRAFT I HAVE USED.

HERE COMES THE LADY: LET HER WITNESS IT.

ENTER DESDEMONA

I THINK THIS TALE WOULD WIN MY DAUGHTER TOO.

GOOD BRABANTIO, TAKE UP THIS MANGLED MATTER AT THE BEST: MEN DO THEIR BROKEN WEAPONS RATHER USE THAN THEIR BARE HANDS.

I PRAY YOU HEAR HER SPEAK. IF SHE CONFESS THAT SHE WAS HALF THE WOOER, DESTRUCTION ON MY HEAD, IF MY BAD BLAME LIGHT ON THE MAN.

COME HITHER, GENTLE MISTRESS. DO YOU PERCEIVE IN ALL THIS COMPANY WHERE MOST YOU OWE OBEDIENCE?

MY NOBLE FATHER, I DO PERCEIVE HERE A DIVIDED DUTY.

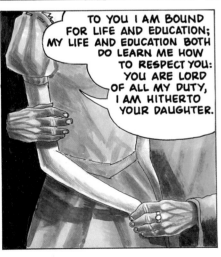

TO YOU I AM BOUND FOR LIFE AND EDUCATION; MY LIFE AND EDUCATION BOTH DO LEARN ME HOW TO RESPECT YOU: YOU ARE LORD OF ALL MY DUTY, I AM HITHERTO YOUR DAUGHTER.

BUT HERE'S MY HUSBAND; AND SO MUCH DUTY AS MY MOTHER SHOWED TO YOU, PREFERRING YOU BEFORE HER FATHER, SO MUCH I CHALLENGE THAT I MAY PROFESS DUE TO THE MOOR, MY LORD.

GOD BE WITH YOU: I HAVE DONE.

PLEASE IT YOUR GRACE ON TO THE STATE AFFAIRS. I HAD RATHER TO ADOPT A CHILD THAN GET IT.

COME HITHER, MOOR: I HERE DO GIVE THEE THAT WITH ALL MY HEART WHICH, BUT THOU HAST ALREADY, WITH ALL MY HEART I WOULD KEEP FROM THEE.

FOR YOUR SAKE, JEWEL, I AM GLAD AT SOUL, I HAVE NO OTHER CHILD, FOR THY ESCAPE WOULD TEACH ME TYRANNY TO HANG CLOGS ON THEM.

I HAVE DONE, MY LORD.

19

LET ME SPEAK LIKE YOURSELF AND LAY A SENTENCE WHICH AS A GRISE OR STEP MAY HELP THESE LOVERS INTO YOUR FAVOUR.

WHEN REMEDIES ARE PAST THE GRIEFS ARE ENDED, BY SEEING THE WORST, WHICH LATE ON HOPES DEPENDED.

TO MOURN A MISCHIEF THAT IS PAST AND GONE IS THE NEXT WAY TO DRAW NEW MISCHIEF ON.

WHAT CANNOT BE PRESERVED WHEN FORTUNE TAKES, PATIENCE HER INJURY A MOCKERY MAKES. THE ROBBED THAT SMILES STEALS SOMETHING FROM THE THIEF; HE ROBS HIMSELF THAT SPENDS A BOOTLESS GRIEF.

SO LET THE TURK OF CYPRUS US BEGUILE, WE LOSE IT NOT SO LONG AS WE CAN SMILE; HE BEARS THE SENTENCE WELL THAT NOTHING BEARS BUT THE FREE COMFORT WHICH FROM THENCE HE HEARS;

BUT HE BEARS BOTH THE SENTENCE AND THE SORROW THAT, TO PAY GRIEF, MUST OF POOR PATIENCE BORROW. THESE SENTENCES, TO SUGAR OR TO GALL, BEING STRONG ON BOTH SIDES, ARE EQUIVOCAL.

BUT WORDS ARE WORDS; I NEVER YET DID HEAR THAT THE BRUISED HEART WAS PIERCED THROUGH THE EAR.

I HUMBLY BESEECH YOU PROCEED TO TH'AFFAIRS OF STATE.

THE TURK WITH A MOST MIGHTY PREPARATION MAKES FOR CYPRUS. OTHELLO, THE FORTITUDE OF THE PLACE IS BEST KNOWN TO YOU;

AND THOUGH WE HAVE THERE A SUBSTITUTE OF MOST ALLOWED SUFFICIENCY, YET OPINION, A MORE SOVEREIGN MISTRESS OF EFFECTS, THROWS A MORE SAFER VOICE ON YOU.

YOU MUST THEREFORE BE CONTENT TO SLUBBER THE GLOSS OF YOUR NEW FORTUNES WITH THIS MORE STUBBORN AND BOISTEROUS EXPEDITION.

THE TYRANT, CUSTOM, MOST GRAVE SENATORS, HATH MADE THE FLINTY AND STEEL COUCH OF WAR MY THRICE-DRIVEN BED OF DOWN. I DO AGNIZE A NATURAL AND PROMPT ALACRITY I FIND IN HARDNESS; AND DO UNDERTAKE THESE PRESENT WARS AGAINST THE OTTOMITES.

MOST HUMBLY, THEREFORE, BENDING TO YOUR STATE, I CRAVE DISPOSITION FOR MY WIFE, DUE REFERENCE OF PLACE AND EXHIBITION, WITH SUCH ACCOMMODATION AND BESORT AS LEVELS WITH HER BREEDING.

IF YOU PLEASE, BE'T AT HER FATHER'S.

I'LL NOT HAVE IT SO.

NOR I.

NOR I: I WOULD NOT THERE RESIDE, TO PUT MY FATHER IN IMPATIENT THOUGHTS BY BEING IN HIS EYE.

MOST GRACIOUS DUKE, TO MY UNFOLDING LEND YOUR PROSPEROUS EAR, AND LET ME FIND A CHARTER IN YOUR VOICE TO ASSIST MY SIMPLENESS.

WHAT WOULD YOU, DESDEMONA?

THAT I DID LOVE THE MOOR TO LIVE WITH HIM, MY DOWNRIGHT VIOLENCE AND STORM OF FORTUNES MAY TRUMPET TO THE WORLD. MY HEART'S SUBDUED EVEN TO THE VERY QUALITY OF MY LORD.

I SAW OTHELLO'S VISAGE IN HIS MIND, AND TO HIS HONOURS AND HIS VALIANT PARTS DID I MY SOUL AND FORTUNES CONSECRATE.

SO THAT, DEAR LORDS, IF I BE LEFT BEHIND A MOTH OF PEACE, AND HE GO TO THE WAR, THE RITES FOR WHICH I LOVE HIM ARE BEREFT ME, AND I A HEAVY INTERIM SHALL SUPPORT BY HIS DEAR ABSENCE.

LET ME GO WITH HIM.

LET HER HAVE YOUR VOICE. VOUCH WITH ME, HEAVEN, I THEREFORE BEG IT NOT TO PLEASE THE PALATE OF MY APPETITE, NOR TO COMPLY WITH HEAT— THE YOUNG AFFECTS IN ME DEFUNCT— BUT TO BE FREE AND BOUNTEOUS TO HER MIND.

AND HEAVEN DEFEND YOUR GOOD SOULS THAT YOU THINK I WILL YOUR SERIOUS AND GREAT BUSINESS SCANT FOR SHE IS WITH ME.

21

HONEST IAGO, MY DESDEMONA MUST I LEAVE TO THEE. I PRITHEE LET THY WIFE ATTEND ON HER, AND BRING THEM AFTER IN THE BEST ADVANTAGE.

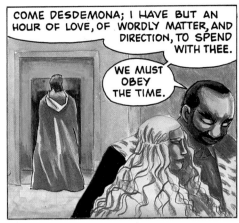

COME DESDEMONA; I HAVE BUT AN HOUR OF LOVE, OF WORDLY MATTER, AND DIRECTION, TO SPEND WITH THEE.

WE MUST OBEY THE TIME.

IAGO.

WHAT SAY'ST THOU, NOBLE HEART?

WHAT WILL I DO, THINK'ST THOU?

WHY, GO TO BED AND SLEEP.

I WILL INCONTINENTLY DROWN MYSELF.

IF THOU DOST I SHALL NEVER LOVE THEE AFTER. WHY, THOU SILLY GENTLEMAN!

IT IS SILLINESS TO LIVE, WHEN TO LIVE IS TORMENT: AND THEN HAVE WE A PRESCRIPTION TO DIE, WHEN DEATH IS OUR PHYSICIAN.

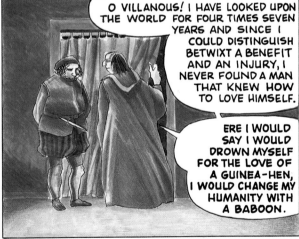

O VILLANOUS! I HAVE LOOKED UPON THE WORLD FOR FOUR TIMES SEVEN YEARS AND SINCE I COULD DISTINGUISH BETWIXT A BENEFIT AND AN INJURY, I NEVER FOUND A MAN THAT KNEW HOW TO LOVE HIMSELF.

ERE I WOULD SAY I WOULD DROWN MYSELF FOR THE LOVE OF A GUINEA-HEN, I WOULD CHANGE MY HUMANITY WITH A BABOON.

WHAT SHOULD I DO? I CONFESS IT IS MY SHAME TO BE SO FOND, BUT IT IS NOT IN MY VIRTUE TO AMEND IT.

VIRTUE? A FIG!

'TIS IN OURSELVES THAT WE ARE THUS, OR THUS. OUR BODIES ARE OUR GARDENS TO THE WHICH OUR WILLS ARE GARDENERS.

SO THAT IF WE WILL PLANT NETTLES OR SOW LETTUCE, SET HYSSOP AND WEED UP THYME, SUPPLY IT WITH ONE GENDER OF HERBS OR DISTRACT IT WITH MANY—EITHER TO HAVE IT STERILE WITH IDLENESS OR MANURED WITH INDUSTRY— WHY, THE POWER AND CORRIGIBLE AUTHORITY OF THIS LIES IN OUR WILLS.

IF THE BALANCE OF OUR LIVES HAD NOT ONE SCALE OF REASON TO POISE ANOTHER OF SENSUALITY, THE BLOOD AND BASENESS OF OUR NATURES WOULD CONDUCT US TO MOST PREPOSTEROUS CONCLUSIONS.

BUT WE HAVE REASON TO COOL OUR RAGING MOTIONS, OUR CARNAL STINGS, OUR UNBITTED LUSTS: WHEREOF I TAKE THIS THAT YOU CALL LOVE, TO BE A SECT OR SCION.

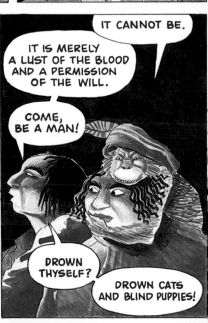

IT CANNOT BE.

IT IS MERELY A LUST OF THE BLOOD AND A PERMISSION OF THE WILL.

COME, BE A MAN!

DROWN THYSELF?

DROWN CATS AND BLIND PUPPIES!

I HAVE PROFESSED ME THY FRIEND, AND I CONFESS ME KNIT TO THY DESERVING WITH CABLES OF PERDURABLE TOUGHNESS. I COULD NEVER BETTER STEAD THEE THAN NOW.

PUT MONEY IN THY PURSE:

FOLLOW THOU THESE WARS, DEFEAT THY FAVOUR WITH AN USURPED BEARD. I SAY PUT MONEY IN THY PURSE: IT CANNOT BE THAT DESDEMONA SHOULD LONG CONTINUE HER LOVE TO THE MOOR

—PUT MONEY IN THY PURSE—

NOR HE HIS TO HER. IT WAS A VIOLENT COMMENCEMENT IN HER, AND THOU SHALT SEE AN ANSWERABLE SEQUESTRATION: PUT BUT MONEY IN THY PURSE.

THESE MOORS ARE CHANGEABLE IN THEIR WILLS: FILL THY PURSE WITH MONEY. THE FOOD THAT TO HIM NOW IS AS LUSCIOUS AS LOCUSTS SHALL BE TO HIM SHORTLY AS BITTER AS COLOQUINTIDA. SHE MUST CHANGE FOR YOUTH. WHEN SHE IS SATED WITH HIS BODY SHE WILL FIND THE ERRORS OF HER CHOICE: SHE MUST HAVE CHANGE, SHE MUST.

THEREFORE PUT MONEY IN THY PURSE.

IF THOU WILT NEEDS DAMN THYSELF, DO IT A MORE DELICATE WAY THAN DROWNING.

MAKE ALL THE MONEY THOU CANST.

IF SANCTIMONY AND A FRAIL VOW BETWIXT AN ERRING BARBARIAN AND A SUPER-SUBTLE VENETIAN BE NOT TOO HARD FOR MY WITS AND ALL THE TRIBE OF HELL, THOU SHALT ENJOY HER. THEREFORE MAKE MONEY.

A POX OF DROWNING THYSELF! IT IS CLEAN OUT OF THE WAY. SEEK THOU RATHER TO BE HANGED IN COMPASSING THY JOY THAN TO BE DROWNED AND GO WITHOUT HER.

WILT THOU BE FAST TO MY HOPES, IF I DEPEND ON THE ISSUE?

THOU ART SURE OF ME. GO, MAKE MONEY!

I HAVE TOLD THEE OFTEN, AND I RETELL THEE AGAIN AND AGAIN, I HATE THE MOOR.

MY CAUSE IS HEARTED: THINE HATH NO LESS REASON. LET US BE CONJUNCTIVE IN OUR REVENGE AGAINST HIM.

IF THOU CANST CUCKOLD HIM, THOU DOST THYSELF A PLEASURE, ME A SPORT.

THERE ARE MANY EVENTS IN THE WOMB OF TIME, WHICH WILL BE DELIVERED.

TRAVERSE, GO, PROVIDE THY MONEY! WE WILL HAVE MORE OF THIS TOMORROW.

ADIEU.

WHERE SHALL WE MEET I'TH'MORNING?

AT MY LODGING.

I'LL BE WITH THEE BETIMES.

GO TO, FAREWELL.

DO YOU HEAR, RODERIGO?

WHAT SAY YOU?

NO MORE OF DROWNING, DO YOU HEAR?

I AM CHANGED.

GO TO, FAREWELL. PUT MONEY ENOUGH IN YOUR PURSE.

I'LL SELL ALL MY LAND.

THUS DO I EVER MAKE MY FOOL MY PURSE: FOR I MINE OWN GAINED KNOWLEDGE SHOULD PROFANE, IF I WOULD TIME EXPEND WITH SUCH A SNIPE BUT FOR MY SPORT AND PROFIT.

I HATE THE MOOR. AND IT IS THOUGHT ABROAD THAT 'TWIXT MY SHEETS HE'S DONE MY OFFICE.

I KNOW NOT IF'T BE TRUE – BUT I, FOR MERE SUSPICION IN THAT KIND, WILL DO AS IF FOR SURETY.

HE HOLDS ME WELL: THE BETTER SHALL MY PURPOSE WORK ON HIM.

CASSIO'S A PROPER MAN: LET ME SEE NOW; TO GET HIS PLACE AND TO PLUME UP MY WILL IN DOUBLE KNAVERY...

HOW? HOW? LET'S SEE...

AFTER SOME TIME, TO ABUSE OTHELLO'S EAR THAT HE IS TOO FAMILIAR WITH HIS WIFE... HE HATH A PERSON AND A SMOOTH DISPOSE TO BE SUSPECTED, FRAMED TO MAKE WOMEN FALSE.

THE MOOR IS OF A FREE AND OPEN NATURE, THAT THINKS MEN HONEST THAT BUT SEEM TO BE SO, AND WILL AS TENDERLY BE LED BY THE NOSE AS ASSES ARE.

I HAVE'T. IT IS ENGENDERED. HELL AND NIGHT MUST BRING THIS MONSTROUS BIRTH TO THE WORLD'S LIGHT.

ENTER GENTLEMAN

OUR WARS ARE DONE: THE DESPERATE TEMPEST HATH SO BANGED THE TURKS THAT THEIR DESIGNMENT HALTS. A NOBLE SHIP OF VENICE HATH SEEN A GRIEVOUS WRACK AND SUFFERANCE ON MOST PART OF THEIR FLEET.

HOW! IS THIS TRUE?

THE SHIP IS HERE PUT IN, A VERONESA; MICHAEL CASSIO, LIEUTENANT TO THE WARLIKE MOOR, OTHELLO, IS COME ON SHORE; THE MOOR HIMSELF'S AT SEA, AND IS IN FULL COMMISSION HERE FOR CYPRUS.

I AM GLAD ON'T; 'TIS A WORTHY GOVERNOR.

BUT THIS SAME CASSIO, THOUGH HE SPEAK OF COMFORT TOUCHING THE TURKISH LOSS, YET HE LOOKS SADLY AND PRAYS THE MOOR BE SAFE; FOR THEY WERE PARTED WITH FOUL AND VIOLENT TEMPEST.

PRAY HEAVEN HE BE: FOR I HAVE SERVED HIM AND THE MAN COMMANDS LIKE A FULL SOLDIER. LET'S TO THE SEA-SIDE, HO!

AS WELL TO SEE THE VESSEL THAT'S COME IN, AS TO THROW OUT OUR EYES FOR BRAVE OTHELLO—EVEN TILL WE MAKE THE MAIN AND TH'AERIAL BLUE AN INDISTINCT REGARD.

COME LET'S DO SO; FOR EVERY MINUTE IS EXPECTANCY OF MORE ARRIVANCE.

ENTER CASSIO

THANKS, YOU THE VALIANT OF THIS WARLIKE ISLE THAT SO APPROVE THE MOOR! O, LET THE HEAVENS GIVE HIM DEFENCE AGAINST THE ELEMENTS, FOR I HAVE LOST HIM ON A DANGEROUS SEA.

IS HE WELL SHIPPED?

HIS BARK IS STOUTLY TIMBERED, AND HIS PILOT OF VERY EXPERT AND APPROVED ALLOWANCE; THEREFORE MY HOPES, NOT SURFEITED TO DEATH, STAND IN BOLD CURE.

A SAIL! A SAIL! A SAIL!

WHAT NOISE?

THE TOWN IS EMPTY; ON THE BROW O'TH'SEA STAND RANKS OF PEOPLE AND THEY CRY A SAIL.

MY HOPES DO SHAPE HIM FOR THE GOVERNOR.

THEY DO DISCHARGE THEIR SHOT OF COURTESY: OUR FRIENDS AT LEAST.

I PRAY YOU, SIR, GO FORTH AND GIVE US TRUTH WHO'TIS THAT IS ARRIVED.

I SHALL.

BUT, GOOD LIEUTENANT, IS YOUR GENERAL WIVED?

MOST FORTUNATELY: HE HATH ACHIEVED A MAID THAT PARAGONS DESCRIPTION AND WILD FAME; ONE THAT EXCELS THE QUIRKS OF BLAZONING PENS, AND IN TH'ESSENTIAL VESTURE OF CREATION DOES TIRE THE INGENER.

HOW NOW? WHO HAS PUT IN?

'TIS ONE IAGO, ANCIENT TO THE GENERAL.

HE'S HAD MOST FAVOURABLE AND HAPPY SPEED: TEMPESTS THEMSELVES, HIGH SEAS AND HOWLING WINDS, THE GUTTERED ROCKS AND CONGREGATED SANDS, TRAITORS ENSCARPED TO CLOG THE GUILTLESS KEEL, AS HAVING SENSE OF BEAUTY, DO OMIT THEIR MORTAL NATURES, LETTING GO SAFELY BY THE DIVINE DESDEMONA.

WHAT IS SHE?

SHE THAT I SPAKE OF, OUR GREAT CAPTAIN'S CAPTAIN, LEFT IN THE CONDUCT OF THE BOLD IAGO, WHOSE FOOTING HERE ANTICIPATES OUR THOUGHTS A SE'NNIGHT'S SPEED. GREAT JOVE, OTHELLO GUARD, AND SWELL HIS SAIL WITH THINE OWN POWERFUL BREATH, THAT HE MAY BLESS THIS BAY WITH HIS TALL SHIP;

MAKE LOVE'S QUICK PANTS IN DESDEMONA'S ARMS, GIVE RENEWED FIRE TO OUR EXTINCTED SPIRITS, AND BRING ALL CYPRUS COMFORT.

ENTER DESDEMONA, EMILIA, IAGO, RODERIGO, ATTENDANTS

O, BEHOLD, THE RICHES OF THE SHIP IS COME ON SHORE!

YOU MEN OF CYPRUS, LET HER HAVE YOUR KNEES. HAIL TO THEE, LADY! AND THE GRACE OF HEAVEN, BEFORE, BEHIND THEE, AND ON EVERY HAND, ENWHEEL THEE ROUND.

I THANK YOU, VALIANT CASSIO.

 WHAT TIDINGS CAN YOU TELL ME OF MY LORD?

HE IS NOT YET ARRIVED; NOR KNOW I AUGHT BUT THAT HE'S WELL, AND WILL BE SHORTLY HERE.

 O, BUT I FEAR! HOW LOST YOU COMPANY?

THE GREAT CONTENTION OF THE SEA AND SKIES PARTED OUR FELLOWSHIP.

 A SAIL! A SAIL!

BUT HARK, A SAIL!

 THEY GIVE THE GREETING TO THE CITADEL: THIS LIKEWISE IS A FRIEND.

SEE FOR THE NEWS.

 GOOD ANCIENT, YOU ARE WELCOME. WELCOME, MISTRESS.

LET IT NOT GALL YOUR PATIENCE, GOOD IAGO, THAT I EXTEND MY MANNERS. 'TIS MY BREEDING THAT GIVES ME THIS BOLD SHOW OF COURTESY.

SIR, WOULD SHE GIVE YOU SO MUCH OF HER LIPS AS OF HER TONGUE SHE OFT BESTOWS ON ME, YOU'D HAVE ENOUGH.

ALAS, SHE HAS NO SPEECH.

 IN FAITH, TOO MUCH!

 I FIND IT STILL, WHEN I HAVE LIST TO SLEEP. MARRY, BEFORE YOUR LADYSHIP, I GRANT, SHE PUTS HER TONGUE A LITTLE IN HER HEART AND CHIDES WITH THINKING.

 YOU HAVE LITTLE CAUSE TO SAY SO.

COME ON, COME ON, YOU ARE PICTURES OUT OF DOORS, BELLS IN YOUR PARLOURS, WILD-CATS IN YOUR KITCHENS, SAINTS IN YOUR INJURIES, DEVILS BEING OFFENDED, PLAYERS IN YOUR HOUSEWIFERY, AND HOUSEWIVES IN YOUR BEDS.

O, FIE UPON THEE, SLANDERER!

NAY, IT IS TRUE, OR ELSE I AM A TURK: YOU RISE TO PLAY AND GO TO BED TO WORK.

YOU SHALL NOT WRITE MY PRAISE!

NO, LET ME NOT.

WHAT WOULDST THOU WRITE OF ME, IF THOU SHOULDST PRAISE ME?

O, GENTLE LADY, DO NOT PUT ME TO'T, FOR I AM NOTHING IF NOT CRITICAL.

COME ON, ASSAY—

THERE'S ONE GONE TO THE HARBOUR?

AY, MADAM.

I AM NOT MERRY, BUT I DO BEGUILE THE THING I AM BY SEEMING OTHERWISE.

COME, HOW WOULDST THOU PRAISE ME?

I AM ABOUT IT, BUT INDEED MY INVENTION COMES FROM MY PATE AS BIRDLIME DOES FROM FRIEZE—IT PLUCKS OUT BRAINS AND ALL. BUT MY MUSE LABOURS, AND THUS SHE IS DELIVERED.

IF SHE BE FAIR AND WISE, FAIRNESS AND WIT, THE ONE'S FOR USE, THE OTHER USETH IT.

WELL PRAISED! HOW IF SHE BE BLACK AND WITTY?

IF SHE BE BLACK, AND THERETO HAVE A WIT, SHE'LL FIND A WHITE, THAT SHALL HER BLACKNESS FIT.

WORSE AND WORSE.

HOW IF FAIR AND FOOLISH?

SHE NEVER YET WAS FOOLISH THAT WAS FAIR, FOR EVEN HER FOLLY HELPED HER TO AN HEIR.

THESE ARE OLD FOND PARADOXES TO MAKE FOOLS LAUGH I'TH'ALEHOUSE. WHAT MISERABLE PRAISE HAST THOU FOR HER THAT'S FOUL AND FOOLISH?

THERE'S NONE SO FOUL AND FOOLISH THEREUNTO, BUT DOES FOUL PRANKS WHICH FAIR AND WISE ONES DO.

O HEAVY IGNORANCE! THOU PRAISEST THE WORST BEST. BUT WHAT PRAISE COULDST THOU BESTOW ON A DESERVING WOMAN INDEED? ONE THAT IN THE AUTHORITY OF HER MERIT DID JUSTLY PUT ON THE VOUCH OF VERY MALICE ITSELF?

SHE THAT WAS EVER FAIR AND NEVER PROUD, HAD TONGUE AT WILL, AND YET WAS NEVER LOUD; NEVER LACKED GOLD, AND YET WENT NEVER GAY; FLED FROM HER WISH, AND YET SAID 'NOW I MAY'; SHE THAT BEING ANGERED, HER REVENGE BEING NIGH, BADE HER WRONG STAY, AND HER DISPLEASURE FLY; SHE THAT IN WISDOM NEVER WAS SO FRAIL TO CHANGE THE COD'S HEAD FOR THE SALMON'S TAIL; SHE THAT COULD THINK AND NE'ER DISCLOSE HER MIND: SEE SUITORS FOLLOWING AND NOT LOOK BEHIND: SHE WAS A WIGHT IF EVER SUCH WIGHT WERE—

TO DO WHAT?

TO SUCKLE FOOLS AND CHRONICLE SMALL BEER.

O, MOST LAME AND IMPOTENT CONCLUSION! DO NOT LEARN OF HIM, EMILIA, THOUGH HE BE THY HUSBAND.

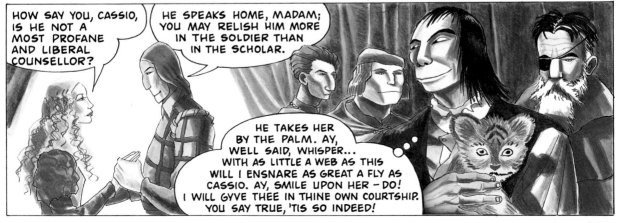

HOW SAY YOU, CASSIO, IS HE NOT A MOST PROFANE AND LIBERAL COUNSELLOR?

HE SPEAKS HOME, MADAM; YOU MAY RELISH HIM MORE IN THE SOLDIER THAN IN THE SCHOLAR.

HE TAKES HER BY THE PALM. AY, WELL SAID, WHISPER... WITH AS LITTLE A WEB AS THIS WILL I ENSNARE AS GREAT A FLY AS CASSIO. AY, SMILE UPON HER – DO! I WILL GYVE THEE IN THINE OWN COURTSHIP. YOU SAY TRUE, 'TIS SO INDEED!

IF SUCH TRICKS AS THESE STRIP YOU OUT OF YOUR LIEUTENANTRY, IT HAD BEEN BETTER YOU HAD NOT KISSED YOUR THREE FINGERS SO OFT, WHICH NOW AGAIN YOU ARE MOST APT TO PLAY THE SIR IN.

VERY GOOD: WELL KISSED, AN EXCELLENT COURTESY! 'TIS SO INDEED! YET AGAIN YOUR FINGERS TO YOUR LIPS? WOULD THEY WERE CLYSTER-PIPES FOR YOUR SAKE!

THE MOOR! I KNOW HIS TRUMPET.

'TIS TRULY SO.

LET'S MEET HIM AND RECEIVE HIM.

LO, WHERE HE COMES!

O, MY FAIR WARRIOR!

MY DEAR OTHELLO!

IT GIVES ME WONDER GREAT AS MY CONTENT TO SEE YOU HERE BEFORE ME. O, MY SOUL'S JOY! IF AFTER EVERY TEMPEST COME SUCH CALMS, MAY THE WINDS BLOW TILL THEY HAVE WAKENED DEATH, AND LET THE LABOURING BARK CLIMB HILLS OF SEAS, OLYMPUS-HIGH, AND DUCK AGAIN AS LOW AS HELL'S FROM HEAVEN.

IF IT WERE NOW TO DIE, 'TWERE NOW TO BE MOST HAPPY; FOR I FEAR MY SOUL HATH HER CONTENT SO ABSOLUTE, THAT NOT ANOTHER COMFORT LIKE TO THIS SUCCEEDS IN UNKNOWN FATE.

THE HEAVENS FORBID BUT THAT OUR LOVES AND COMFORTS SHOULD INCREASE, EVEN AS OUR DAYS DO GROW.

AMEN TO THAT, SWEET POWERS!

I CANNOT SPEAK ENOUGH OF THIS CONTENT; IT STOPS ME HERE.

IT IS TOO MUCH OF JOY.

AND THIS, AND THIS THE GREATEST DISCORDS BE THAT E'ER OUR HEARTS SHALL MAKE.

O, YOU ARE WELL TUNED NOW! BUT I'LL SET DOWN THE PEGS THAT MAKE THIS MUSIC, AS HONEST AS I AM.

COME, LET'S TO THE CASTLE.

HOW DOES MY OLD ACQUAINTANCE OF THIS ISLE?

NEWS, FRIENDS; OUR WARS ARE DONE; THE TURKS ARE DROWNED!

HONEY, YOU SHALL BE WELL-DESIRED IN CYPRUS: I HAVE FOUND GREAT LOVE AMONGST THEM. O, MY SWEET, I PRATTLE OUT OF FASHION AND I DOTE IN MINE OWN COMFORTS.

I PRITHEE, GOOD IAGO, GO TO THE BAY AND DISEMBARK MY COFFERS; BRING THOU THE MASTER TO THE CITADEL: HE IS A GOOD ONE AND HIS WORTHINESS DOES CHALLENGE MUCH RESPECT.

COME, DESDEMONA.

35

ONCE MORE, WELL MET AT CYPRUS!

DO THOU MEET ME PRESENTLY AT THE HARBOUR.

COME HITHER, IF THOU BE'ST VALIANT – AS THEY SAY BASE MEN BEING IN LOVE HAVE THEN A NOBILITY IN THEIR NATURES MORE THAN IS NATIVE TO THEM – LIST ME. THE LIEUTENANT TONIGHT WATCHES ON THE COURT OF GUARD. FIRST, I MUST TELL THEE THIS:

DESDEMONA IS DIRECTLY IN LOVE WITH HIM.

WITH HIM? WHY 'TIS NOT POSSIBLE!

LAY THY FINGER THUS, AND LET THY SOUL BE INSTRUCTED. MARK ME WITH WHAT VIOLENCE SHE FIRST LOVED THE MOOR, BUT FOR BRAGGING AND TELLING HER FANTASTICAL LIES.

AND WILL SHE LOVE HIM STILL FOR PRATING? LET NOT THY DISCREET HEART THINK IT. HER EYE MUST BE FED. AND WHAT DELIGHT SHALL SHE HAVE TO LOOK ON THE DEVIL?

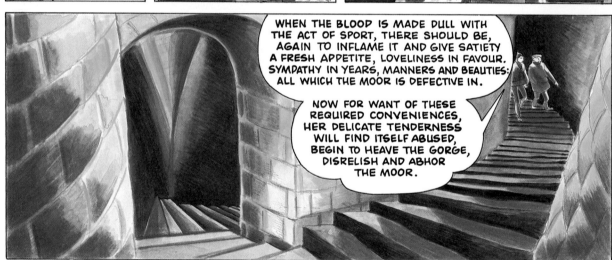

WHEN THE BLOOD IS MADE DULL WITH THE ACT OF SPORT, THERE SHOULD BE, AGAIN TO INFLAME IT AND GIVE SATIETY A FRESH APPETITE, LOVELINESS IN FAVOUR. SYMPATHY IN YEARS, MANNERS AND BEAUTIES: ALL WHICH THE MOOR IS DEFECTIVE IN.

NOW FOR WANT OF THESE REQUIRED CONVENIENCES, HER DELICATE TENDERNESS WILL FIND ITSELF ABUSED, BEGIN TO HEAVE THE GORGE, DISRELISH AND ABHOR THE MOOR.

VERY NATURE WILL INSTRUCT HER IN IT AND COMPEL HER TO SOME SECOND CHOICE. NOW SIR, THIS GRANTED – AS IT IS A MOST PREGNANT AND UNFORCED POSITION – WHO STANDS SO EMINENT IN THE DEGREE OF THIS FORTUNE AS CASSIO DOES? –

A KNAVE VERY VOLUBLE, NO FURTHER CONSCIONABLE THAN IN PUTTING ON THE MERE FORM OF CIVIL AND HUMANE SEEMING FOR THE BETTER COMPASS OF HIS SALT AND MOST HIDDEN LOOSE AFFECTION.

WHY, NONE; WHY, NONE - A SLIPPER AND SUBTLE KNAVE, A FINDER OUT OF OCCASIONS; THAT HAS AN EYE CAN STAMP AND COUNTERFEIT ADVANTAGES, THOUGH TRUE ADVANTAGE NEVER PRESENT ITSELF; A DEVILISH KNAVE!

BESIDES, THE KNAVE IS HANDSOME, YOUNG, AND HATH ALL THOSE REQUISITES IN HIM THAT FOLLY AND GREEN MINDS LOOK AFTER. A PESTILENT COMPLETE KNAVE; AND THE WOMAN HATH FOUND HIM ALREADY.

I CANNOT BELIEVE THAT IN HER! SHE'S FULL OF MOST BLESSED CONDITION.

BLESSED FIG'S END!

THE WINE SHE DRINKS IS MADE OF GRAPES.

IF SHE HAD BEEN BLESSED SHE WOULD NEVER HAVE LOVED THE MOOR.

BLESSED PUDDING! DIDST THOU NOT SEE HER PADDLE WITH THE PALM OF HIS HAND? DIDST NOT MARK THAT?

YES, THAT I DID: BUT THAT WAS BUT COURTESY.

LECHERY, BY THIS HAND: AN INDEX AND OBSCURE PROLOGUE TO THE HISTORY OF LUST AND FOUL THOUGHTS. THEY MET SO NEAR WITH THEIR LIPS THAT THEIR BREATHS EMBRACED TOGETHER.

VILLAINOUS THOUGHTS, RODERIGO! WHEN THESE MUTUALITIES SO MARSHAL THE WAY, HARD AT HAND COMES THE MASTER AND MAIN EXERCISE, TH'INCORPORATE CONCLUSION. PISH! BUT, SIR, BE YOU RULED BY ME.

I HAVE BROUGHT YOU FROM VENICE. WATCH YOU TONIGHT: FOR THE COMMAND -I'LL LAY'T UPON YOU. CASSIO KNOWS YOU NOT; I'LL NOT BE FAR FROM YOU.

DO YOU FIND SOME OCCASION TO ANGER CASSIO, EITHER BY SPEAKING TOO LOUD, OR TAINTING HIS DISCIPLINE, OR FROM WHAT OTHER CAUSE YOU PLEASE, WHICH THE TIME SHALL MORE FAVOURABLY MINISTER.

WELL....

SIR, HE'S RASH AND VERY SUDDEN IN CHOLER, AND HAPLY MAY STRIKE AT YOU: PROVOKE HIM THAT HE MAY, FOR EVEN OUT OF THAT WILL I CAUSE THESE OF CYPRUS TO MUTINY, WHOSE QUALIFICATION SHALL COME INTO NO TRUE TASTE AGAIN BUT BY THE DISPLANTING OF CASSIO.

SO SHALL YOU HAVE A SHORTER JOURNEY TO YOUR DESIRES BY THE MEANS I SHALL THEN HAVE TO PREFER THEM—AND THE IMPEDIMENT MOST PROFITABLY REMOVED, WITHOUT THE WHICH THERE WERE NO EXPECTATION OF OUR PROSPERITY.

I WILL DO THIS IF YOU CAN BRING IT TO ANY OPPORTUNITY.

I WARRANT THEE. MEET ME BY AND BY AT THE CITADEL. I MUST FETCH HIS NECESSARIES ASHORE.

FAREWELL.

ADIEU.

THAT CASSIO LOVES HER I DO WELL BELIEVE'T: THAT SHE LOVES HIM, 'TIS APT AND OF GREAT CREDIT. THE MOOR— HOW BE IT THAT I ENDURE HIM NOT— IS OF A CONSTANT, LOVING, NOBLE NATURE, AND I DARE THINK HE'LL PROVE TO DESDEMONA A MOST DEAR HUSBAND.

NOW I DO LOVE HER TOO; NOT OUT OF ABSOLUTE LUST— THOUGH PERADVENTURE I DO STAND ACCOUNTANT FOR AS GREAT A SIN—

BUT PARTLY LED TO DIET MY REVENGE, FOR THAT I DO SUSPECT THE LUSTY MOOR HATH LEAPED INTO MY SEAT,

IAGO IS MOST HONEST.

MICHAEL, GOOD NIGHT. TOMORROW WITH YOUR EARLIEST LET ME HAVE SPEECH WITH YOU.

GOOD MICHAEL, LOOK YOU TO THE GUARD TONIGHT. LET'S TEACH OURSELVES THAT HONOURABLE STOP, NOT TO OUTSPORT DISCRETION.

IAGO HATH DIRECTION WHAT TO DO; BUT, NOTWITHSTANDING, WITH MY PERSONAL EYE WILL I LOOK TO'T.

COME MY DEAR LOVE, THE PURCHASE MADE, THE FRUITS ARE TO ENSUE: THAT PROFIT'S YET TO COME 'TWEEN ME AND YOU.

GOOD NIGHT.

WELCOME, IAGO. WE MUST TO THE WATCH.

NOT THIS HOUR, LIEUTENANT; 'TIS NOT YET TEN O'THE CLOCK. OUR GENERAL CAST US THUS EARLY FOR THE LOVE OF HIS DESDEMONA; WHO LET US NOT THEREFORE BLAME. HE HATH NOT YET MADE WANTON THE NIGHT WITH HER... AND SHE IS SPORT FOR JOVE.

SHE IS A MOST EXQUISITE LADY.

AND, I'LL WARRANT HER, FULL OF GAME.

INDEED, SHE'S A MOST FRESH AND DELICATE CREATURE.

WHAT AN EYE SHE HAS! METHINKS IT SOUNDS A PARLEY TO PROVOCATION.

AN INVITING EYE— AND YET METHINKS RIGHT MODEST.

AND WHEN SHE SPEAKS, IS IT NOT AN ALARUM TO LOVE?

SHE IS INDEED PERFECTION.

WELL, HAPPINESS TO THEIR SHEETS! COME LIEUTENANT, I HAVE A STOUP OF WINE; AND HERE WITHOUT ARE A BRACE OF CYPRUS GALLANTS THAT WOULD FAIN HAVE A MEASURE TO THE HEALTH OF BLACK OTHELLO.

NOT TONIGHT, GOOD IAGO!

I HAVE VERY POOR AND UNHAPPY BRAINS FOR DRINKING. I COULD WELL WISH COURTESY WOULD INVENT SOME OTHER CUSTOM OF ENTERTAINMENT.

O, THEY ARE OUR FRIENDS!

BUT ONE CUP; I'LL DRINK FOR YOU.

I HAVE DRUNK BUT ONE CUP TONIGHT, AND THAT WAS CRAFTILY QUALIFIED TOO; AND BEHOLD WHAT INNOVATION IT MAKES HERE.

I AM UNFORTUNATE IN THE INFIRMITY AND DARE NOT TASK MY WEAKNESS WITH ANY MORE.

WHAT MAN! 'TIS A NIGHT OF REVELS! THE GALLANTS DESIRE IT.

WHERE ARE THEY?

HERE, AT THE DOOR: I PRAY YOU CALL THEM IN.

I'LL DO'T, BUT IT DISLIKES ME.

IF I CAN FASTEN BUT ONE CUP UPON HIM, WITH THAT WHICH HE HATH DRUNK TONIGHT ALREADY, HE'LL BE AS FULL OF QUARREL AND OFFENCE AS MY YOUNG MISTRESS' DOG. NOW MY SICK FOOL RODERIGO, WHOM LOVE HATH TURNED ALMOST THE WRONG SIDE OUT, TO DESDEMONA HATH TONIGHT CAROUSED POTATIONS POTTLE-DEEP...

AND HE'S TO WATCH.

THREE ELSE OF CYPRUS, NOBLE SWELLING SPIRITS— THAT HOLD THEIR HONOURS IN A WARY DISTANCE, THE VERY ELEMENTS OF THIS WARLIKE ISLE — HAVE I TONIGHT FLUSTERED WITH FLOWING CUPS — AND THEY WATCH TOO. NOW 'MONGST THIS FLOCK OF DRUNKARDS, AM I TO PUT OUR CASSIO IN SOME ACTION THAT MAY OFFEND THE ISLE...

BUT HERE THEY COME. IF CONSEQUENCE DO BUT APPROVE MY DREAM, MY BOAT SAILS FREELY BOTH WITH WIND AND STREAM.

'FORE GOD, THEY HAVE GIVEN ME A ROUSE ALREADY.

GOOD FAITH, A LITTLE ONE; NOT PAST A PINT, AS I AM A SOLDIER.

SOME WINE, HO!

AND LET ME THE CANAKIN CLINK, CLINK; AND LET ME THE CANAKIN CLINK; A SOLDIER'S A MAN— O, MAN'S LIFE'S BUT A SPAN; WHY, THEN, LET A SOLDIER DRINK.

SOME WINE, BOYS!

'FORE GOD, AN EXCELLENT SONG.

I LEARNED IT IN ENGLAND, WHERE INDEED THEY ARE MOST POTENT IN POTTING.

YOUR DANE, YOUR GERMAN AND YOUR SWAG-BELLIED HOLLANDER — DRINK, HO! — ARE NOTHING TO YOUR ENGLISH.

IS YOUR ENGLISHMAN SO EXPERT IN HIS DRINKING?

WHY, HE DRINKS YOU WITH FACILITY YOUR DANE DEAD DRUNK; HE SWEATS NOT TO OVERTHROW YOUR ALMAINE; HE GIVES YOUR HOLLANDER A VOMIT, ERE THE NEXT POTTLE CAN BE FILLED.

TO THE HEALTH OF OUR GENERAL!

I AM FOR IT, LIEUTENANT; AND I'LL DO YOU JUSTICE!

O, SWEET ENGLAND!

KING STEPHEN WAS AND-A WORTHY PEER, HIS BREECHES COST HIM BUT A CROWN; HE HELD THEM SIXPENCE ALL TOO DEAR; WITH THAT HE CALLED THE TAILOR LOWN. HE WAS A WIGHT OF HIGH RENOWN, AND THOU ART BUT OF LOW DEGREE; 'TIS PRIDE THAT PULLS THE COUNTRY DOWN; THEN TAKE THINE AULD CLOAK ABOUT THEE.

SOME WINE, HO!

'FORE GOD, THIS IS A MORE EXQUISITE SONG THAN THE OTHER.

WILL YOU HEAR IT AGAIN?

NO, FOR I HOLD HIM TO BE UNWORTHY OF HIS PLACE THAT DOES THOSE THINGS. WELL GOD'S ABOVE ALL; AND THERE BE SOULS MUST BE SAVED, AND THERE BE SOULS MUST NOT BE SAVED.

IT'S TRUE, GOOD LIEUTENANT.

FOR MY OWN PART— NO OFFENCE TO THE GENERAL, NOR ANY MAN OF QUALITY— I HOPE TO BE SAVED.

AND SO DO I TOO, LIEUTENANT.

AY, BUT, BY YOUR LEAVE, NOT BEFORE ME. THE LIEUTENANT IS TO BE SAVED BEFORE THE ANCIENT. LET'S HAVE NO MORE OF THIS; LET'S TO OUR AFFAIRS. GOD FORGIVE US OUR SINS.

GENTLEMEN, LET'S LOOK TO OUR BUSINESS. DO NOT THINK, GENTLEMEN, I AM DRUNK...

THIS IS MY ANCIENT, THIS IS MY RIGHT HAND—AND THIS IS MY LEFT. I AM NOT DRUNK NOW. I CAN STAND WELL ENOUGH AND I SPEAK WELL ENOUGH.

EXCELLENT WELL.

WHY, VERY WELL; YOU MUST NOT THINK THEN THAT I AM DRUNK.

TO TH' PLATFORM, MASTERS; COME, LET'S SET THE WATCH.

YOU SEE THIS FELLOW THAT IS GONE BEFORE: HE IS A SOLDIER FIT TO STAND BY CAESAR AND GIVE DIRECTION; AND DO BUT SEE HIS VICE: 'TIS TO HIS VIRTUE A JUST EQUINOX, THE ONE AS LONG AS TH'OTHER. 'TIS PITY OF HIM. I FEAR THE TRUST OTHELLO PUTS IN HIM, ON SOME ODD TIME OF HIS INFIRMITY, WILL SHAKE THIS ISLAND.

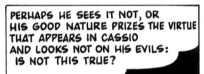

BUT IS HE OFTEN THUS?

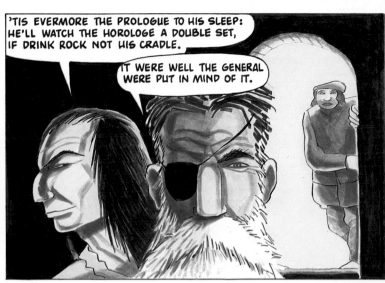

'TIS EVERMORE THE PROLOGUE TO HIS SLEEP: HE'LL WATCH THE HOROLOGE A DOUBLE SET, IF DRINK ROCK NOT HIS CRADLE.

IT WERE WELL THE GENERAL WERE PUT IN MIND OF IT.

PERHAPS HE SEES IT NOT, OR HIS GOOD NATURE PRIZES THE VIRTUE THAT APPEARS IN CASSIO AND LOOKS NOT ON HIS EVILS: IS NOT THIS TRUE?

HOW NOW, RODERIGO! I PRAY YOU AFTER THE LIEUTENANT GO!

AND 'TIS GREAT PITY THAT THE NOBLE MOOR SHOULD HAZARD SUCH A PLACE AS HIS OWN SECOND WITH ONE OF AN INGRAFT INFIRMITY. IT WERE AN HONEST ACTION TO SAY SO TO THE MOOR.

NOT I, FOR THIS FAIR ISLAND! I DO LOVE CASSIO WELL AND WOULD DO MUCH TO CURE HIM OF THIS EVIL.

HELP! HELP!

BUT HARK, WHAT NOISE?

ZOUNDS! YOU ROGUE! YOU RASCAL!

WHAT'S THE MATTER, LIEUTENANT?

A KNAVE TEACH ME MY DUTY? I'LL BEAT THE KNAVE INTO A TWIGGEN-BOTTLE!

BEAT ME?

DOST THOU PRATE ROGUE?

NAY, GOOD LIEUTENANT; I PRAY YOU, SIR, HOLD YOUR HAND.

LET ME GO, SIR, OR I'LL KNOCK YOU O'ER THE MAZZARD.

COME, COME— YOU'RE DRUNK.

DRUNK?

AWAY, I SAY; GO OUT AND CRY A MUTINY.

HOW COMES IT, MICHAEL, YOU ARE THUS FORGOT?

I PRAY YOU PARDON ME: I CANNOT SPEAK.

WORTHY MONTANO, YOU WERE WONT TO BE CIVIL: THE GRAVITY AND STILLNESS OF YOUR YOUTH THE WORLD HATH NOTED; AND YOUR NAME IS GREAT IN MOUTHS OF WISEST CENSURE. WHAT'S THE MATTER THAT YOU UNLACE YOUR REPUTATION THUS AND SPEND YOUR RICH OPINION FOR THE NAME OF A NIGHT-BRAWLER? GIVE ME ANSWER TO IT.

WORTHY OTHELLO, I AM HURT TO DANGER.

YOUR OFFICER, IAGO, CAN INFORM YOU—WHILE I SPARE SPEECH WHICH SOMETHING NOW OFFENDS ME— OF ALL THAT I DO KNOW; NOR KNOW I AUGHT BY ME THAT'S SAID OR DONE AMISS THIS NIGHT, UNLESS SELF-CHARITY BE SOMETIMES A VICE, AND TO DEFEND OURSELVES IT BE A SIN WHEN VIOLENCE ASSAILS US.

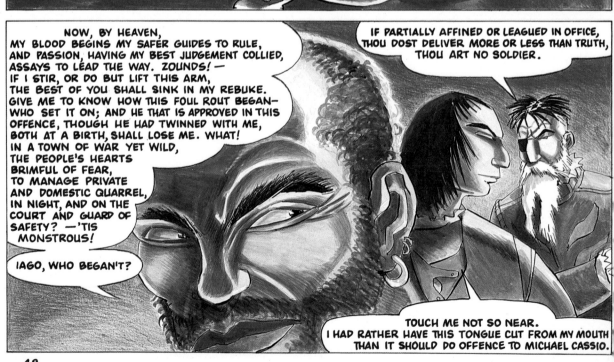

NOW, BY HEAVEN, MY BLOOD BEGINS MY SAFER GUIDES TO RULE, AND PASSION, HAVING MY BEST JUDGEMENT COLLIED, ASSAYS TO LEAD THE WAY. ZOUNDS!— IF I STIR, OR DO BUT LIFT THIS ARM, THE BEST OF YOU SHALL SINK IN MY REBUKE. GIVE ME TO KNOW HOW THIS FOUL ROUT BEGAN— WHO SET IT ON; AND HE THAT IS APPROVED IN THIS OFFENCE, THOUGH HE HAD TWINNED WITH ME, BOTH AT A BIRTH, SHALL LOSE ME. WHAT! IN A TOWN OF WAR YET WILD, THE PEOPLE'S HEARTS BRIMFUL OF FEAR, TO MANAGE PRIVATE AND DOMESTIC QUARREL, IN NIGHT, AND ON THE COURT AND GUARD OF SAFETY? —'TIS MONSTROUS!

IAGO, WHO BEGAN'T?

IF PARTIALLY AFFINED OR LEAGUED IN OFFICE, THOU DOST DELIVER MORE OR LESS THAN TRUTH, THOU ART NO SOLDIER.

TOUCH ME NOT SO NEAR. I HAD RATHER HAVE THIS TONGUE CUT FROM MY MOUTH THAN IT SHOULD DO OFFENCE TO MICHAEL CASSIO.

YET, I PERSUADE MYSELF, TO SPEAK THE TRUTH SHALL NOTHING WRONG HIM. THIS IT IS, GENERAL. MONTANO AND MYSELF BEING IN SPEECH, THERE COMES A FELLOW CRYING OUT FOR HELP, AND CASSIO FOLLOWING WITH DETERMINED SWORD TO EXECUTE UPON HIM. SIR, THIS GENTLEMAN STEPS IN TO CASSIO AND ENTREATS HIS PAUSE: MYSELF THE CRYING FELLOW DID PURSUE LEST BY HIS CLAMOUR — AS IT SO FELL OUT— THE TOWN MIGHT FALL IN FRIGHT. HE, SWIFT OF FOOT, OUTRAN MY PURPOSE, AND I RETURNED — THE RATHER FOR THAT I HEARD THE CLINK AND FALL OF SWORDS, AND CASSIO HIGH IN OATH — WHICH TILL TONIGHT I NE'ER MIGHT SAY BEFORE.

WHEN I CAME BACK—FOR THIS WAS BRIEF— I FOUND THEM CLOSE TOGETHER AT BLOW AND THRUST, EVEN AS AGAIN THEY WERE WHEN YOU YOURSELF DID PART THEM. MORE OF THIS MATTER CANNOT I REPORT— BUT MEN ARE MEN; THE BEST SOMETIMES FORGET. THOUGH CASSIO DID SOME LITTLE WRONG TO HIM, AS MEN IN RAGE STRIKE THOSE THAT WISH THEM BEST, YET SURELY CASSIO, I BELIEVE, RECEIVED FROM HIM THAT FLED SOME STRANGE INDIGNITY WHICH PATIENCE COULD NOT PASS.

I KNOW, IAGO, THY HONESTY AND LOVE DOTH MINCE THIS MATTER, MAKING IT LIGHT TO CASSIO.

CASSIO, I LOVE THEE, BUT NEVER MORE BE OFFICER OF MINE.

LOOK, IF MY GENTLE LOVE BE NOT RAISED UP.

I'LL MAKE THEE AN EXAMPLE!

WHAT IS THE MATTER, DEAR?

ALL'S WELL NOW, SWEETING: COME AWAY TO BED.

SIR, FOR YOUR HURTS MYSELF WILL BE YOUR SURGEON.

IAGO, LOOK WITH CARE ABOUT THE TOWN AND SILENCE THOSE WHOM THIS VILE BRAWL DISTRACTED.

COME, DESDEMONA, 'TIS THE SOLDIERS' LIFE TO HAVE THEIR BALMY SLUMBERS WAKED WITH STRIFE.

WHAT, ARE YOU HURT, LIEUTENANT?

AY, PAST ALL SURGERY.

MARRY, GOD FORBID!

REPUTATION! REPUTATION! REPUTATION!

O, I HAVE LOST MY REPUTATION!

I HAVE LOST THE IMMORTAL PART OF MYSELF, AND WHAT REMAINS IS BESTIAL.

MY REPUTATION, IAGO, MY REPUTATION!

AS I AM AN HONEST MAN I THOUGHT YOU HAD RECEIVED SOME BODILY WOUND: THERE IS MORE OF SENSE IN THAT THAN IN REPUTATION. REPUTATION IS AN IDLE AND MOST FALSE IMPOSITION; OFT GOT WITHOUT MERIT AND LOST WITHOUT DESERVING. YOU HAVE LOST NO REPUTATION AT ALL, UNLESS YOU REPUTE YOURSELF SUCH A LOSER.

WHAT, MAN! THERE ARE WAYS TO RECOVER THE GENERAL AGAIN.

YOU ARE BUT NOW CAST IN HIS MOOD —A PUNISHMENT MORE IN POLICY THAN IN MALICE— EVEN SO AS ONE WOULD BEAT HIS OFFENCELESS DOG TO AFFRIGHT AN IMPERIOUS LION. SUE TO HIM AGAIN, AND HE'S YOURS.

I WILL RATHER SUE TO BE DESPISED THAN TO DECEIVE SO GOOD A COMMANDER WITH SO SLIGHT, SO DRUNKEN AND SO INDISCREET AN OFFICER.

DRUNK! AND SPEAK PARROT! AND SQUABBLE! SWAGGER! SWEAR!

AND DISCOURSE FUSTIAN WITH ONE'S OWN SHADOW! O, THOU INVISIBLE SPIRIT OF WINE, IF THOU HAST NO NAME TO BE KNOWN BY, LET US CALL THEE DEVIL!

WHAT WAS HE THAT YOU FOLLOWED WITH YOUR SWORD? WHAT HAD HE DONE TO YOU?

I KNOW NOT.

IS'T POSSIBLE?

I REMEMBER A MASS OF THINGS BUT NOTHING DISTINCTLY. A QUARREL, BUT NOTHING WHEREFORE. O GOD, THAT MEN SHOULD PUT AN ENEMY IN THEIR MOUTHS TO STEAL AWAY THEIR BRAINS!

THAT WE SHOULD WITH JOY, PLEASANCE, REVEL AND APPLAUSE, TRANSFORM OURSELVES INTO BEASTS!

WHY, BUT YOU ARE NOW WELL ENOUGH. HOW CAME YOU THUS RECOVERED?

IT HATH PLEASED THE DEVIL DRUNKENNESS TO GIVE PLACE TO THE DEVIL WRATH: ONE UNPERFECTNESS SHOWS ME ANOTHER, TO MAKE ME FRANKLY DESPISE MYSELF.

COME, YOU ARE TOO SEVERE A MORALLER. AS THE TIME, THE PLACE AND THE CONDITION OF THIS COUNTRY STANDS, I COULD HEARTILY WISH THIS HAD NOT BEFALLEN: BUT SINCE IT IS AS IT IS, MEND IT FOR YOUR OWN GOOD.

I WILL ASK HIM FOR MY PLACE AGAIN— HE SHALL TELL ME I AM A DRUNKARD. HAD I AS MANY MOUTHS AS HYDRA, SUCH AN ANSWER WOULD STOP THEM ALL.

TO BE NOW A SENSIBLE MAN, BY AND BY A FOOL, AND PRESENTLY A BEAST! O, STRANGE! EVERY INORDINATE CUP IS UNBLESSED AND THE INGREDIENCE IS A DEVIL.

COME, COME; GOOD WINE IS A GOOD FAMILIAR CREATURE IF IT BE WELL USED: EXCLAIM NO MORE AGAINST IT.

AND, GOOD LIEUTENANT, I THINK YOU THINK I LOVE YOU.

I HAVE WELL APPROVED IT, SIR.

I, DRUNK.

YOU OR ANY MAN LIVING MAY BE DRUNK AT A TIME, MAN. I TELL YOU WHAT YOU SHALL DO. OUR GENERAL'S WIFE IS NOW THE GENERAL. I MAY SAY SO IN THIS RESPECT, FOR THAT HE HATH DEVOTED AND GIVEN UP HIMSELF TO THE CONTEMPLATION, MARK, AND DENOTEMENT OF HER PARTS AND GRACES.

CONFESS YOURSELF FREELY TO HER; IMPORTUNE HER HELP TO PUT YOU IN YOUR PLACE AGAIN. SHE IS OF SO FREE, SO KIND, SO APT, SO BLESSED A DISPOSITION, SHE HOLDS IT A VICE, IN HER GOODNESS, NOT TO DO MORE THAN SHE IS REQUESTED.

THIS BROKEN JOINT BETWEEN YOU AND HER HUSBAND, ENTREAT HER TO SPLINTER; AND MY FORTUNES AGAINST ANY LAY WORTH NAMING, THIS CRACK OF YOUR LOVE SHALL GROW STRONGER THAN IT WAS BEFORE.

YOU ADVISE ME WELL.

I PROTEST, IN THE SINCERITY OF LOVE AND HONEST KINDNESS.

I THINK IT FREELY; AND BETIMES IN THE MORNING I WILL BESEECH THE VIRTUOUS DESDEMONA TO UNDERTAKE FOR ME.

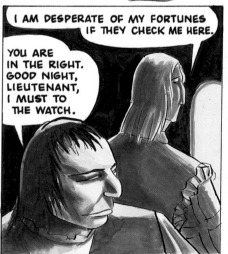

I AM DESPERATE OF MY FORTUNES IF THEY CHECK ME HERE.

YOU ARE IN THE RIGHT. GOOD NIGHT, LIEUTENANT, I MUST TO THE WATCH.

GOOD NIGHT, HONEST IAGO.

AND WHAT'S HE THEN THAT SAYS I PLAY THE VILLAIN? WHEN THIS ADVICE IS FREE I GIVE, AND HONEST, PROBAL TO THINKING, AND INDEED THE COURSE TO WIN THE MOOR AGAIN. FOR 'TIS MOST EASY TH'INCLINING DESDEMONA TO SUBDUE IN ANY HONEST SUIT.

SHE'S FRAMED AS FRUITFUL AS THE FREE ELEMENTS; AND THEN FOR HER TO WIN THE MOOR—WERE'T TO RENOUNCE HIS BAPTISM, ALL SEALS AND SYMBOLS OF REDEEMÈD SIN—HIS SOUL IS SO ENFETTERED TO HER LOVE, THAT SHE MAY MAKE, UNMAKE, DO WHAT SHE LIST, EVEN AS HER APPETITE SHALL PLAY THE GOD WITH HIS WEAK FUNCTION.

HOW AM I THEN A VILLAIN TO COUNSEL CASSIO TO THIS PARALLEL COURSE DIRECTLY TO HIS GOOD?

DIVINITY OF HELL! WHEN DEVILS WILL THE BLACKEST SINS PUT ON, THEY DO SUGGEST AT FIRST WITH HEAVENLY SHOWS AS I DO NOW. FOR WHILES THIS HONEST FOOL PLIES DESDEMONA TO REPAIR HIS FORTUNES AND SHE FOR HIM PLEADS STRONGLY TO THE MOOR, I'LL POUR THIS PESTILENCE INTO HIS EAR —THAT SHE REPEALS HIM FOR HER BODY'S LUST...

AND BY HOW MUCH SHE STRIVES TO DO HIM GOOD, SHE SHALL UNDO HER CREDIT WITH THE MOOR. SO WILL I TURN HER VIRTUE INTO PITCH, AND OUT OF HER OWN GOODNESS MAKE THE NET THAT SHALL ENMESH THEM ALL.

HOW NOW, RODERIGO?

I DO FOLLOW HERE IN THE CHASE, NOT LIKE A HOUND THAT HUNTS, BUT ONE THAT FILLS UP THE CRY. MY MONEY IS ALMOST SPENT; I HAVE BEEN TONIGHT EXCEEDINGLY WELL CUDGELLED; AND I THINK THE ISSUE WILL BE, I SHALL HAVE SO MUCH EXPERIENCE FOR MY PAINS; AND SO, WITH NO MONEY AT ALL AND A LITTLE MORE WIT, RETURN AGAIN TO VENICE.

HOW POOR ARE THEY THAT HAVE NOT PATIENCE! WHAT WOUND DID EVER HEAL BUT BY DEGREES? THOU KNOW'ST WE WORK BY WIT AND NOT BY WITCHCRAFT, AND WIT DEPENDS ON DILATORY TIME.

DOES'T NOT GO WELL? CASSIO HATH BEATEN THEE, AND THOU BY THAT SMALL HURT HATH CASHIERED CASSIO.

THOUGH OTHER THINGS GROW FAIR AGAINST THE SUN, YET FRUITS THAT BLOSSOM FIRST WILL FIRST BE RIPE. CONTENT THYSELF AWHILE.

BY TH'MASS, 'TIS MORNING: PLEASURE AND ACTION MAKE THE HOURS SEEM SHORT.

RETIRE THEE. GO WHERE THOU ART BILLETED. AWAY, I SAY, THOU SHALT KNOW MORE HEREAFTER.

NAY, GET THEE GONE!

TWO THINGS ARE TO BE DONE. MY WIFE MUST MOVE FOR CASSIO TO HER MISTRESS: I'LL SET HER ON. MYSELF THE WHILE TO DRAW THE MOOR APART, AND BRING HIM JUMP WHEN HE MAY CASSIO FIND SOLICITING HIS WIFE.

AY, THAT'S THE WAY. DULL NOT DEVICE BY COLDNESS AND DELAY.

BUT MASTERS, HERE'S MONEY FOR YOU: AND THE GENERAL SO LIKES YOUR MUSIC THAT HE DESIRES YOU, FOR LOVE'S SAKE...

TO MAKE NO MORE NOISE WITH IT.

WELL, SIR, WE WILL NOT.

IF YOU HAVE ANY MUSIC THAT MAY NOT BE HEARD, TO'T AGAIN. BUT, AS THEY SAY, TO HEAR MUSIC THE GENERAL DOES NOT GREATLY CARE.

THEN PUT UP YOUR PIPES IN YOUR BAG, FOR I'LL AWAY.

GO!

VANISH INTO AIR!

AWAY!

WE HAVE NONE SUCH, SIR.

DOST THOU HEAR, MINE HONEST FRIEND?

NO, I HEAR NOT YOUR HONEST FRIEND: I HEAR YOU!

PRITHEE KEEP UP THY QUILLETS!

THERE'S A POOR PIECE OF GOLD FOR THEE. IF THE GENTLEWOMAN THAT ATTENDS THE GENERAL'S WIFE BE STIRRING, TELL HER THERE'S ONE CASSIO ENTREATS HER A LITTLE FAVOUR OF SPEECH. WILT THOU DO THIS?

SHE IS STIRRING, SIR. IF SHE WILL STIR HITHER, I SHALL SEEM TO NOTIFY UNTO HER.

DO, GOOD MY FRIEND.

IN HAPPY TIME, IAGO.

YOU HAVE NOT BEEN ABED THEN?

WHY, NO: THE DAY HAD BROKE BEFORE WE PARTED. I HAVE MADE BOLD, IAGO, TO SEND IN TO YOUR WIFE. MY SUIT TO HER IS THAT SHE WILL TO VIRTUOUS DESDEMONA PROCURE ME SOME ACCESS.

I'LL SEND HER TO YOU PRESENTLY; AND I'LL DEVISE A MEAN TO DRAW THE MOOR OUT OF THE WAY, THAT YOUR CONVERSE AND BUSINESS MAY BE MORE FREE.

I HUMBLY THANK YOU FOR'T.

BE THOU ASSURED, GOOD CASSIO, I WILL DO ALL MY ABILITIES IN THY BEHALF.

GOOD MADAM, DO: I WARRANT IT GRIEVES MY HUSBAND AS IF THE CASE WERE HIS.

O, THAT'S AN HONEST FELLOW! DO NOT DOUBT, CASSIO, BUT I WILL HAVE MY LORD AND YOU AGAIN AS FRIENDLY AS YOU WERE.

ACT III, SCENE III

BOUNTEOUS MADAM, WHATEVER SHALL BECOME OF MICHAEL CASSIO, HE'S NEVER ANYTHING BUT YOUR TRUE SERVANT.

I KNOW'T: I THANK YOU. YOU DO LOVE MY LORD; YOU HAVE KNOWN HIM LONG, AND BE YOU WELL ASSURED HE SHALL IN STRANGENESS STAND NO FARTHER OFF THAN IN POLITIC DISTANCE.

AY, BUT, LADY, THAT POLICY MAY EITHER LAST SO LONG, OR FEED UPON SUCH NICE AND WATERISH DIET, OR BREED ITSELF SO OUT OF CIRCUMSTANCE, THAT I BEING ABSENT, AND MY PLACE SUPPLIED, MY GENERAL WILL FORGET MY LOVE AND SERVICE.

DO NOT DOUBT THAT. BEFORE EMILIA HERE, I GIVE THEE WARRANT OF THY PLACE.

ASSURE THEE, IF I DO VOW A FRIENDSHIP, I'LL PERFORM IT TO THE LAST ARTICLE. MY LORD SHALL NEVER REST. I'LL WATCH HIM TAME AND TALK HIM OUT OF PATIENCE; HIS BED SHALL SEEM A SCHOOL, HIS BOARD A SHRIFT; I'LL INTERMINGLE EVERYTHING HE DOES WITH CASSIO'S SUIT.

THEREFORE BE MERRY, CASSIO, FOR THY SOLICITOR SHALL RATHER DIE THAN GIVE THY CAUSE AWAY.

MADAM, HERE COMES MY LORD.

MADAM, I'LL TAKE MY LEAVE.

WHY, STAY AND HEAR ME SPEAK.

MADAM, NOT NOW: I AM VERY ILL AT EASE —UNFIT FOR MINE OWN PURPOSES.

WELL, DO YOUR DISCRETION.

HA! I LIKE NOT THAT.

WHAT DOST THOU SAY?

NOTHING, MY LORD; OR IF— I KNOW NOT WHAT.

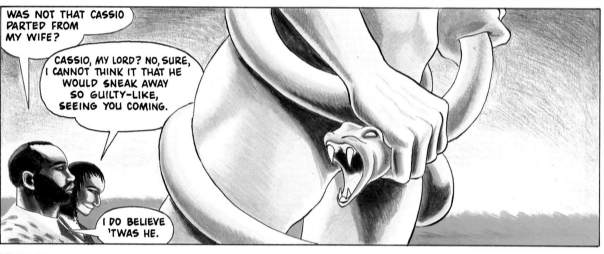

WAS NOT THAT CASSIO PARTED FROM MY WIFE?

CASSIO, MY LORD? NO, SURE, I CANNOT THINK IT THAT HE WOULD SNEAK AWAY SO GUILTY-LIKE, SEEING YOU COMING.

I DO BELIEVE 'TWAS HE.

HOW NOW, MY LORD? I HAVE BEEN TALKING WITH A SUITOR HERE, A MAN THAT LANGUISHES IN YOUR DISPLEASURE.

WHO IS'T YOU MEAN?

WHY, YOUR LIEUTENANT, CASSIO. GOOD MY LORD, IF I HAVE ANY GRACE OR POWER TO MOVE YOU, HIS PRESENT RECONCILIATION TAKE. FOR IF HE BE NOT ONE THAT TRULY LOVES YOU, THAT ERRS IN IGNORANCE, AND NOT IN CUNNING, I HAVE NO JUDGEMENT IN AN HONEST FACE.

I PRITHEE CALL HIM BACK.

WENT HE HENCE NOW?

AY, SOOTH; SO HUMBLED THAT HE HATH LEFT PART OF HIS GRIEF WITH ME TO SUFFER WITH HIM.

GOOD LOVE, CALL HIM BACK.

NOT NOW, SWEET DESDEMONA; SOME OTHER TIME.

BUT SHALL'T BE SHORTLY?

THE SOONER, SWEET, FOR YOU.

SHALL'T BE TONIGHT, AT SUPPER?

NO, NOT TONIGHT.

TOMORROW DINNER, THEN?

I SHALL NOT DINE AT HOME. I MEET THE CAPTAINS AT THE CITADEL.

WHY THEN, TOMORROW NIGHT, OR TUESDAY MORN, ON TUESDAY NOON, OR NIGHT; ON WEDNESDAY MORN. I PRITHEE, NAME THE TIME, BUT LET IT NOT EXCEED THREE DAYS. IN FAITH, HE'S PENITENT.

AND YET HIS TRESPASS, IN OUR COMMON REASON (SAVE THAT, THEY SAY, THE WARS MUST MAKE EXAMPLE OUT OF THEIR BEST) IS NOT ALMOST A FAULT T'INCUR A PRIVATE CHECK. WHEN SHALL HE COME? TELL ME, OTHELLO!

I WONDER IN MY SOUL WHAT YOU WOULD ASK ME THAT I SHOULD DENY OR STAND SO MAMMERING ON? WHAT! MICHAEL CASSIO, THAT CAME A-WOOING WITH YOU, AND SO MANY A TIME WHEN I HAVE SPOKE OF YOU DISPRAISINGLY HATH TA'EN YOUR PART— TO HAVE SO MUCH TO DO TO BRING HIM IN?

BY'R LADY, I COULD DO MUCH—

PRITHEE, NO MORE: LET HIM COME WHEN HE WILL; I WILL DENY THEE NOTHING.

WHY, THIS IS NOT A BOON: 'TIS AS I SHOULD ENTREAT YOU WEAR YOUR GLOVES OR FEED ON NOURISHING DISHES, OR KEEP YOU WARM, OR SUE TO YOU TO DO A PECULIAR PROFIT TO YOUR OWN PERSON.

NAY, WHEN I HAVE A SUIT WHEREIN I MEAN TO TOUCH YOUR LOVE INDEED, IT SHALL BE FULL OF POISE AND DIFFICULT WEIGHT, AND FEARFUL TO BE GRANTED.

I WILL DENY THEE NOTHING.

WHEREON, I DO BESEECH THEE GRANT ME THIS; TO LEAVE ME BUT A LITTLE TO MY SELF.

SHALL I DENY YOU? NO; FAREWELL, MY LORD.

FAREWELL, MY DESDEMONA, I'LL COME TO THEE STRAIGHT.

EMILIA, COME.

BE AS YOUR FANCIES TEACH YOU. WHATE'ER YOU BE, I AM OBEDIENT.

EXCELLENT WRETCH! PERDITION CATCH MY SOUL BUT I DO LOVE THEE! AND WHEN I LOVE THEE NOT, CHAOS IS COME AGAIN.

MY NOBLE LORD...

WHAT DOST THOU SAY, IAGO?

DID MICHAEL CASSIO, WHEN YOU WOOED MY LADY, KNOW OF YOUR LOVE?

HE DID, FROM FIRST TO LAST. WHY DOST THOU ASK?

BUT FOR A SATISFACTION OF MY THOUGHT— NO FURTHER HARM.

WHY OF THY THOUGHT, IAGO?

I DID NOT THINK HE HAD BEEN ACQUAINTED WITH HER.

O YES, AND WENT BETWEEN US VERY OFT.

INDEED?

INDEED? AY, INDEED. DISCERN'ST THOU AUGHT IN THAT? IS HE NOT HONEST?

HONEST, MY LORD?

HONEST? AY, HONEST.

MY LORD, FOR AUGHT I KNOW.

WHAT DOST THOU THINK?

THINK, MY LORD?

THINK, MY LORD? BY HEAVEN HE ECHOES ME, AS IF THERE WERE SOME MONSTER IN HIS THOUGHT TOO HIDEOUS TO BE SHOWN.

THOU DOST MEAN SOMETHING. I HEARD THEE SAY, EVEN NOW, THOU LIK'ST NOT THAT, WHEN CASSIO LEFT MY WIFE. WHAT DIDST NOT LIKE? AND WHEN I TOLD THEE HE WAS OF MY COUNSEL IN MY WHOLE COURSE OF WOOING, THOU CRIED'ST "INDEED?" AND DIDST CONTRACT AND PURSE THY BROW TOGETHER, AS IF THOU THEN HAD'ST SHUT UP IN THY BRAIN SOME HORRIBLE CONCEIT.

IF THOU DOST LOVE ME, SHOW ME THY THOUGHT.

MY LORD, YOU KNOW I LOVE YOU.

I THINK THOU DOST: AND FOR I KNOW THOU'RT FULL OF LOVE AND HONESTY, AND WEIGH'ST THY WORDS BEFORE THOU GIV'ST THEM BREATH, THEREFORE THESE STOPS OF THINE FRIGHT ME THE MORE:

FOR SUCH THINGS IN A FALSE DISLOYAL KNAVE ARE TRICKS OF CUSTOM; BUT IN A MAN THAT'S JUST, THEY'RE CLOSE DILATIONS, WORKING FROM THE HEART, THAT PASSION CANNOT RULE.

FOR MICHAEL CASSIO, I DARE BE SWORN, I THINK THAT HE IS HONEST.

I THINK SO TOO.

MEN SHOULD BE WHAT THEY SEEM; OR THOSE THAT BE NOT, WOULD THEY MIGHT SEEM NONE!

CERTAIN, MEN SHOULD BE WHAT THEY SEEM.

WHY, THEN, I THINK CASSIO'S AN HONEST MAN.

NAY, YET THERE'S MORE IN THIS. I PRITHEE SPEAK TO ME AS TO THY THINKINGS, AS THOU DOST RUMINATE, AND GIVE THY WORST OF THOUGHTS THE WORST OF WORDS.

GOOD MY LORD, PARDON ME; THOUGH I AM BOUND TO EVERY ACT OF DUTY, I AM NOT BOUND TO THAT ALL SLAVES ARE FREE TO.

UTTER MY THOUGHTS? WHY SAY THEY ARE VILE AND FALSE? AS WHERE'S THAT PALACE WHEREINTO FOUL THINGS SOMETIMES INTRUDE NOT?

WHO HAS A BREAST SO PURE, BUT SOME UNCLEANLY APPREHENSIONS KEEP LEETS AND LAW-DAYS, AND IN SESSION SIT WITH MEDITATIONS LAWFUL?

THOU DOST CONSPIRE AGAINST THY FRIEND, IAGO, IF THOU BUT THINK'ST HIM WRONGED, AND MAK'ST HIS EAR A STRANGER TO THY THOUGHTS.

I DO BESEECH YOU—THOUGH I PERCHANCE AM VICIOUS IN MY GUESS (AS I CONFESS IT IS MY NATURE'S PLAGUE TO SPY INTO ABUSES, AND OF MY JEALOUSY SHAPE FAULTS THAT ARE NOT)—THAT YOUR WISDOM, FROM ONE THAT SO IMPERFECTLY CONCEITS, WOULD TAKE NO NOTICE, NOR BUILD YOURSELF A TROUBLE OUT OF HIS SCATTERING AND UNSURE OBSERVANCE.

IT WERE NOT FOR YOUR QUIET, NOR YOUR GOOD, NOR FOR MY MANHOOD, HONESTY, AND WISDOM, TO LET YOU KNOW MY THOUGHTS.

WHAT DOST THOU MEAN?

GOOD NAME IN MAN AND WOMAN, DEAR MY LORD, IS THE IMMEDIATE JEWEL OF THEIR SOULS. WHO STEALS MY PURSE, STEALS TRASH; 'TIS SOMETHING, NOTHING; 'TWAS MINE, 'TIS HIS, AND HAS BEEN SLAVE TO THOUSANDS: BUT HE THAT FILCHES FROM ME MY GOOD NAME ROBS ME OF THAT WHICH NOT ENRICHES HIM, AND MAKES ME POOR INDEED.

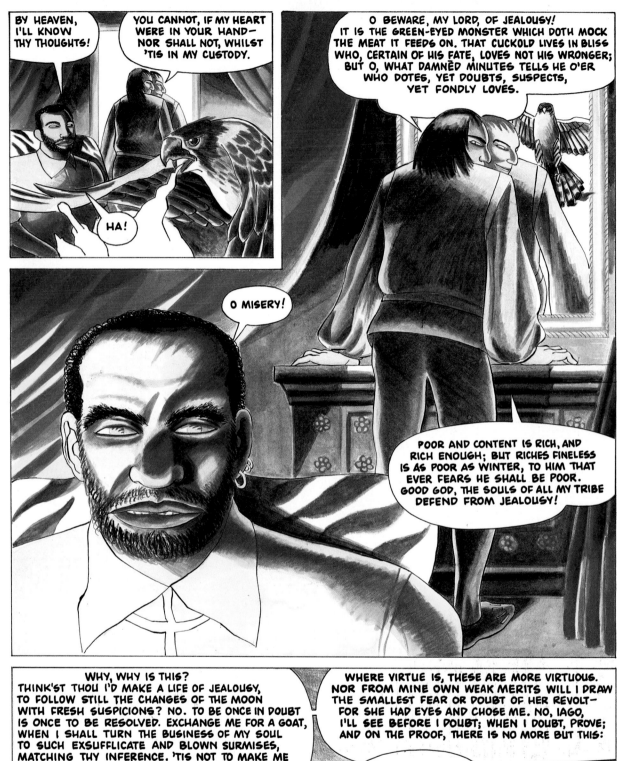

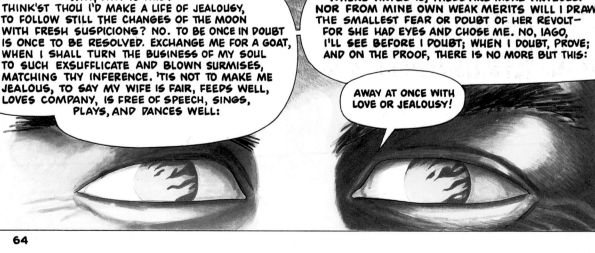

I SEE THIS HATH A LITTLE DASHED YOUR SPIRITS.

NOT A JOT, NOT A JOT.

I'FAITH, I FEAR IT HAS. I HOPE YOU WILL CONSIDER WHAT IS SPOKE COMES FROM MY LOVE. BUT I DO SEE YOU'RE MOVED. I AM TO PRAY YOU, NOT TO STRAIN MY SPEECH TO GROSSER ISSUES, NOR TO LARGER REACH THAN TO SUSPICION.

I WILL NOT.

SHOULD YOU DO SO, MY LORD, MY SPEECH SHOULD FALL INTO SUCH VILE SUCCESS WHICH MY THOUGHTS AIMED NOT AT. CASSIO'S MY WORTHY FRIEND.

MY LORD, I SEE YOU'RE MOVED.

NO, NOT MUCH MOVED. I DO NOT THINK BUT DESDEMONA'S HONEST.

LONG LIVE SHE SO! AND LONG LIVE YOU TO THINK SO!

AND YET, HOW NATURE, ERRING FROM ITSELF—

AY, THERE'S THE POINT!

AS (TO BE BOLD WITH YOU) NOT TO AFFECT MANY PROPOSED MATCHES OF HER OWN CLIME, COMPLEXION, AND DEGREE—WHERETO WE SEE IN ALL THINGS NATURE TENDS—FOH! ONE MAY SMELL IN SUCH, A WILL MOST RANK, FOUL DISPROPORTIONS, THOUGHTS UNNATURAL.

BUT, PARDON ME, I DO NOT IN POSITION DISTINCTLY SPEAK OF HER...

THOUGH I MAY FEAR HER WILL (RECOILING TO HER BETTER JUDGEMENT) MAY FALL TO MATCH YOU WITH HER COUNTRY FORMS, AND HAPPILY REPENT.

FAREWELL, FAREWELL. IF MORE THOU DOST PERCEIVE, LET ME KNOW MORE. SET ON THY WIFE TO OBSERVE.

LEAVE ME, IAGO.

MY LORD, I TAKE MY LEAVE.

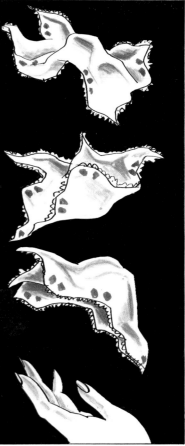

I WILL IN CASSIO'S LODGING LOSE THIS NAPKIN, AND LET HIM FIND IT. TRIFLES LIGHT AS AIR ARE TO THE JEALOUS CONFIRMATIONS STRONG AS PROOF OF HOLY WRIT.

THIS MAY DO SOMETHING. THE MOOR ALREADY CHANGES WITH MY POISON. DANGEROUS CONCEITS ARE IN THEIR NATURES POISONS, WHICH AT THE FIRST ARE SCARCE FOUND TO DISTASTE, BUT, WITH A LITTLE ACT UPON THE BLOOD, BURN LIKE THE MINES OF SULPHUR.

I DID SAY SO: LOOK WHERE HE COMES! NOT POPPY, NOR MANDRAGORA, NOR ALL THE DROWSY SYRUPS OF THE WORLD, SHALL EVER MEDICINE THEE TO THAT SWEET SLEEP WHICH THOU OWED'ST YESTERDAY.

HA! HA! FALSE TO ME!

WHY, HOW NOW, GENERAL? NO MORE OF THAT!

AVAUNT! BE GONE! THOU HAST SET ME ON THE RACK. I SWEAR 'TIS BETTER TO BE MUCH ABUSED, THAN BUT TO KNOW'T A LITTLE.

HOW NOW, MY LORD?

WHAT SENSE HAD I OF HER STOLEN HOURS OF LUST? I SAW'T NOT, THOUGHT IT NOT, IT HARMED NOT ME. I SLEPT THE NEXT NIGHT WELL, FED WELL, WAS FREE AND MERRY. I FOUND NOT CASSIO'S KISSES ON HER LIPS.

HE THAT IS ROBBED, NOT WANTING WHAT IS STOLEN, LET HIM NOT KNOW'T, AND HE'S NOT ROBBED AT ALL.

I AM SORRY TO HEAR THIS.

I HAD BEEN HAPPY IF THE GENERAL CAMP- PIONEERS AND ALL—HAD TASTED HER SWEET BODY, SO I HAD NOTHING KNOWN.

O, NOW, FOR EVER FAREWELL THE TRANQUIL MIND! FAREWELL CONTENT! FAREWELL THE PLUMÈD TROOPS AND THE BIG WARS THAT MAKE AMBITION VIRTUE—O, FAREWELL! FAREWELL THE NEIGHING STEED AND THE SHRILL TRUMP, THE SPIRIT-STIRRING DRUM, TH'EAR-PIERCING FIFE,

THE ROYAL BANNER AND ALL QUALITY, PRIDE, POMP AND CIRCUMSTANCE OF GLORIOUS WAR! AND, O YOU MORTAL ENGINES, WHOSE RUDE THROATS TH'IMMORTAL JOVE'S DREAD CLAMOURS COUNTERFEIT, FAREWELL!

OTHELLO'S OCCUPATION'S GONE!

IS'T POSSIBLE, MY LORD?

VILLAIN, BE SURE THOU PROVE MY LOVE A WHORE; BE SURE OF IT: GIVE ME THE OCULAR PROOF, OR BY THE WORTH OF MINE ETERNAL SOUL, THOU HADST BEEN BETTER HAVE BEEN BORN A DOG THAN ANSWER MY WAKED WRATH!

IS'T COME TO THIS?

MAKE ME TO SEE'T: OR, AT THE LEAST, SO PROVE IT THAT THE PROBATION BEAR NO HINGE NOR LOOP TO HANG A DOUBT ON: OR WOE UPON THY LIFE!

MY NOBLE LORD—

IF THOU DOST SLANDER HER AND TORTURE ME, NEVER PRAY MORE-ABANDON ALL REMORSE! ON HORROR'S HEAD HORRORS ACCUMULATE; DO DEEDS TO MAKE HEAVEN WEEP, ALL EARTH AMAZED: FOR NOTHING CANST THOU TO DAMNATION ADD GREATER THAN THAT!

O GRACE! O HEAVEN DEFEND ME!

ARE YOU A MAN? HAVE YOU A SOUL? OR SENSE? GOD BU'Y YOU: TAKE MINE OFFICE. O WRETCHED FOOL, THAT LOV'ST TO MAKE THINE HONESTY A VICE! O MONSTROUS WORLD! TAKE NOTE, TAKE NOTE, O WORLD-TO BE DIRECT AND HONEST IS NOT SAFE.

I THANK YOU FOR THIS PROFIT, AND FROM HENCE I'LL LOVE NO FRIEND, SITH LOVE BREEDS SUCH OFFENCE.

NAY, STAY: THOU SHOULDST BE HONEST.

I SHOULD BE WISE; FOR HONESTY'S A FOOL AND LOSES THAT IT WORKS FOR.

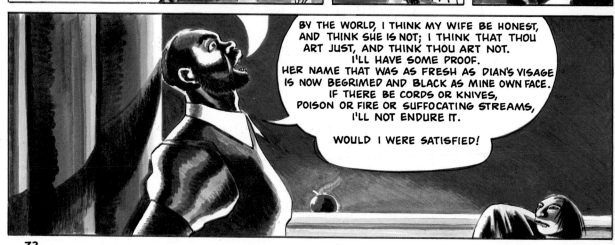

BY THE WORLD, I THINK MY WIFE BE HONEST, AND THINK SHE IS NOT; I THINK THAT THOU ART JUST, AND THINK THOU ART NOT. I'LL HAVE SOME PROOF. HER NAME THAT WAS AS FRESH AS DIAN'S VISAGE IS NOW BEGRIMED AND BLACK AS MINE OWN FACE. IF THERE BE CORDS OR KNIVES, POISON OR FIRE OR SUFFOCATING STREAMS, I'LL NOT ENDURE IT.

WOULD I WERE SATISFIED!

IN SLEEP I HEARD HIM SAY:
"SWEET DESDEMONA, LET US BE WARY,
LET US HIDE OUR LOVES"; AND THEN, SIR,
WOULD HE GRIPE AND WRING MY HAND,
CRY "O SWEET CREATURE!" AND THEN
KISS ME HARD, AS IF HE PLUCKED UP KISSES
BY THE ROOTS, THAT GREW UPON MY LIPS;
THEN LAID HIS LEG OVER MY THIGH,
AND SIGHED AND KISSED, AND THEN CRIED
"CURSÈD FATE THAT GAVE THEE
TO THE MOOR!"

O MONSTROUS! MONSTROUS!

NAY, THIS WAS BUT HIS DREAM.

BUT THIS DENOTED A FOREGONE CONCLUSION.

'TIS A SHREWD DOUBT, THOUGH IT BE BUT A DREAM: AND THIS MAY HELP TO THICKEN OTHER PROOFS THAT DO DEMONSTRATE THINLY.

I'LL TEAR HER ALL TO PIECES!

NAY, BUT BE WISE: YET WE SEE NOTHING DONE, SHE MAY BE HONEST YET. TELL ME BUT THIS: HAVE YOU NOT SOMETIMES SEEN A HANDKERCHIEF, SPOTTED WITH STRAWBERRIES, IN YOUR WIFE'S HAND?

I GAVE HER SUCH A ONE: 'TWAS MY FIRST GIFT.

I KNOW NOT THAT: BUT SUCH A HANDKERCHIEF - I AM SURE IT WAS YOUR WIFE'S - DID I TODAY SEE CASSIO WIPE HIS BEARD WITH.

IF IT BE THAT!

IF IT BE THAT - OR ANY THAT WAS HERS - IT SPEAKS AGAINST HER WITH THE OTHER PROOFS.

O, THAT THE SLAVE HAD FORTY THOUSAND LIVES! ONE IS TOO POOR, TOO WEAK FOR MY REVENGE. NOW DO I SEE 'TIS TRUE. LOOK HERE, IAGO - ALL MY FOND LOVE THUS DO I BLOW TO HEAVEN: 'TIS GONE. ARISE, BLACK VENGEANCE, FROM THY HOLLOW CELL! YIELD UP, O LOVE, THY CROWN AND HEARTED THRONE TO TYRANNOUS HATE! SWELL, BOSOM, WITH THY FRAUGHT, FOR 'TIS OF ASPICS' TONGUES!

YET BE CONTENT.

O BLOOD, BLOOD, BLOOD!

PATIENCE, I SAY: YOUR MIND PERHAPS MAY CHANGE.

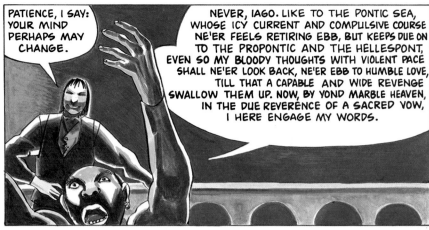

NEVER, IAGO. LIKE TO THE PONTIC SEA, WHOSE ICY CURRENT AND COMPULSIVE COURSE NE'ER FEELS RETIRING EBB, BUT KEEPS DUE ON TO THE PROPONTIC AND THE HELLESPONT, EVEN SO MY BLOODY THOUGHTS WITH VIOLENT PACE SHALL NE'ER LOOK BACK, NE'ER EBB TO HUMBLE LOVE, TILL THAT A CAPABLE AND WIDE REVENGE SWALLOW THEM UP. NOW, BY YOND MARBLE HEAVEN, IN THE DUE REVERENCE OF A SACRED VOW, I HERE ENGAGE MY WORDS.

DO NOT RISE YET.

WITNESS, YOU EVER-BURNING LIGHTS ABOVE, YOU ELEMENTS, THAT CLIP US ROUND ABOUT, WITNESS THAT HERE IAGO DOTH GIVE UP THE EXECUTION OF HIS WIT, HANDS, HEART, TO WRONGED OTHELLO'S SERVICE. LET HIM COMMAND, AND TO OBEY SHALL BE IN ME REMORSE, WHAT BLOODY BUSINESS EVER.

I GREET THY LOVE, NOT WITH VAIN THANKS, BUT WITH ACCEPTANCE BOUNTEOUS; AND WILL UPON THE INSTANT PUT THEE TO'T.

WITHIN THESE THREE DAYS LET ME HEAR THEE SAY THAT CASSIO'S NOT ALIVE.

MY FRIEND IS DEAD; 'TIS DONE AT YOUR REQUEST, BUT LET HER LIVE.

DAMN HER, LEWD MINX! O DAMN HER, DAMN HER! COME GO WITH ME APART. I WILL WITHDRAW TO FURNISH ME WITH SOME SWEET MEANS OF DEATH FOR THE FAIR DEVIL.

NOW ART THOU MY LIEUTENANT.

I AM YOUR OWN FOREVER.

DO YOU KNOW, SIRRAH, WHERE LIEUTENANT CASSIO LIES?

I DARE NOT SAY HE LIES ANYWHERE.

TO TELL YOU WHERE HE LODGES IS TO TELL YOU WHERE I LIE.

CAN ANYTHING BE MADE OF THIS?

WHY, MAN?

HE'S A SOLDIER, AND FOR ONE TO SAY A SOLDIER LIES IS STABBING.

GO TO! WHERE LODGES HE?

I KNOW NOT WHERE HE LODGES, AND FOR ME TO DEVISE A LODGING, AND SAY HE LIES HERE, OR HE LIES THERE, WERE TO LIE IN MINE OWN THROAT.

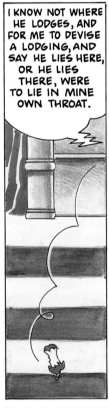

CAN YOU INQUIRE HIM OUT? AND BE EDIFIED BY REPORT?

I WILL CATECHIZE THE WORLD FOR HIM, THAT IS, MAKE QUESTIONS, AND BY THEM ANSWER.

SEEK HIM; BID HIM COME HITHER; TELL HIM I HAVE MOVED MY LORD ON HIS BEHALF, AND HOPE ALL WILL BE WELL.

TO DO THIS IS WITHIN THE COMPASS OF MAN'S WIT, AND THEREFORE I WILL ATTEMPT THE DOING OF IT.

WHERE SHOULD I LOSE THAT HANDKERCHIEF, EMILIA?

I KNOW NOT, MADAM.

76

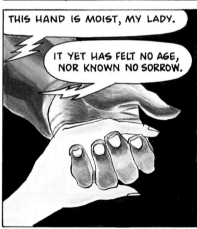
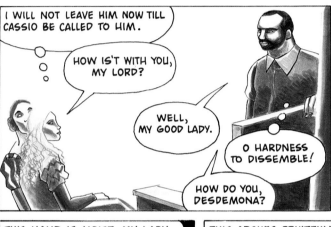

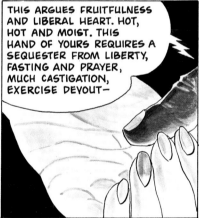

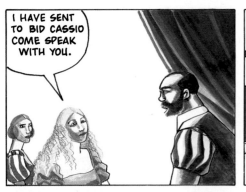

I HAVE SENT TO BID CASSIO COME SPEAK WITH YOU.

I HAVE A SALT AND SORRY RHEUM OFFENDS ME...

LEND ME THY HANDKERCHIEF.

HERE, MY LORD.

THAT WHICH I GAVE YOU.

I HAVE IT NOT ABOUT ME.

NOT?

NO, FAITH, MY LORD.

THAT'S A FAULT. THAT HANDKERCHIEF DID AN EGYPTIAN TO MY MOTHER GIVE: SHE WAS A CHARMER AND COULD ALMOST READ THE THOUGHTS OF PEOPLE. SHE TOLD HER, WHILE SHE KEPT IT, 'TWOULD MAKE HER AMIABLE AND SUBDUE MY FATHER ENTIRELY TO HER LOVE; BUT, IF SHE LOST IT OR MADE A GIFT OF IT, MY FATHER'S EYE SHOULD HOLD HER LOATHÈD, AND HIS SPIRITS SHOULD HUNT AFTER NEW FANCIES. SHE, DYING, GAVE IT ME, AND BID ME, WHEN MY FATE WOULD HAVE ME WIVED, TO GIVE IT HER. I DID SO; AND TAKE HEED ON'T: MAKE IT A DARLING, LIKE YOUR PRECIOUS EYE. TO LOSE OR GIVE'T AWAY WERE SUCH PERDITION AS NOTHING ELSE COULD MATCH.

IS'T POSSIBLE?

'TIS TRUE: THERE'S MAGIC IN THE WEB OF IT. A SIBYL, THAT HAD NUMBERED IN THE WORLD THE SUN TO COURSE TWO HUNDRED COMPASSES, IN HER PROPHETIC FURY SEWED THE WORK: THE WORMS WERE HALLOWED THAT DID BREED THE SILK, AND IT WAS DYED IN MUMMY, WHICH THE SKILFUL CONSERVED OF MAIDENS' HEARTS.

INDEED! IS'T TRUE?

MOST VERITABLE; THEREFORE LOOK TO'T WELL.

THEN WOULD TO GOD THAT I HAD NEVER SEEN IT!

HA! WHEREFORE?

WHY DO YOU SPEAK SO STARTINGLY AND RASH?

IS'T LOST? IS'T GONE? SPEAK: IS'T OUT O'TH'WAY?

HEAVEN BLESS US!

SAY YOU?

IT IS NOT LOST. BUT WHAT AN IF IT WERE?

HOW?

I SAY IT IS NOT LOST.

FETCH'T: LET ME SEE'T.

WHY, SO I CAN, SIR: BUT I WILL NOT NOW. THIS IS A TRICK TO PUT ME FROM MY SUIT. PRAY YOU LET CASSIO BE RECEIVED AGAIN.

FETCH ME THE HANDKERCHIEF: MY MIND MISGIVES.

COME, COME: YOU'LL NEVER MEET A MORE SUFFICIENT MAN.

THE HANDKERCHIEF!

I PRAY, TALK ME OF CASSIO.

THE HANDKERCHIEF!

A MAN THAT ALL HIS TIME HATH FOUNDED HIS GOOD FORTUNES ON YOUR LOVE; SHARED DANGERS WITH YOU—

THE HANDKERCHIEF!

I'FAITH YOU ARE TO BLAME.

ZOUNDS!

IS NOT THIS MAN JEALOUS?

I NE'ER SAW THIS BEFORE. SURE, THERE'S SOME WONDER IN THIS HANDKERCHIEF: I AM MOST UNHAPPY IN THE LOSS OF IT.

'TIS NOT A YEAR OR TWO SHOWS US A MAN. THEY ARE ALL BUT STOMACHS, AND WE ALL BUT FOOD; THEY EAT US HUNGERLY, AND WHEN THEY ARE FULL, THEY BELCH US!

79

LOOK YOU, CASSIO AND MY HUSBAND.

THERE IS NO OTHER WAY: 'TIS SHE MUST DO'T. AND LO, THE HAPPINESS! GO, AND IMPORTUNE HER.

HOW NOW, GOOD CASSIO! WHAT'S THE NEWS WITH YOU?

MADAM, MY FORMER SUIT. I DO BESEECH YOU THAT BY YOUR VIRTUOUS MEANS I MAY AGAIN EXIST AND BE A MEMBER OF HIS LOVE, WHOM I, WITH ALL THE OFFICE OF MY HEART, ENTIRELY HONOUR. I WOULD NOT BE DELAYED. IF MY OFFENCE BE OF SUCH MORTAL KIND THAT NOR MY SERVICE PAST, NOR PRESENT SORROW, NOR PURPOSED MERIT IN FUTURITY, CAN RANSOM ME INTO HIS LOVE AGAIN, BUT TO KNOW SO MUST BE MY BENEFIT: SO SHALL I CLOTHE ME IN A FORCED CONTENT, AND SHUT MYSELF UP IN SOME OTHER COURSE TO FORTUNE'S ALMS.

ALAS, THRICE-GENTLE CASSIO! MY ADVOCATION IS NOT NOW IN TUNE: MY LORD IS NOT MY LORD; NOR SHOULD I KNOW HIM, WERE HE IN FAVOUR AS IN HUMOUR ALTERED.

SO HELP ME EVERY SPIRIT SANCTIFIED AS I HAVE SPOKEN FOR YOU ALL MY BEST, AND STOOD WITHIN THE BLANK OF HIS DISPLEASURE FOR MY FREE SPEECH!

YOU MUST AWHILE BE PATIENT. WHAT I CAN DO, I WILL; AND MORE I WILL, THAN FOR MYSELF I DARE: LET THAT SUFFICE YOU.

IS MY LORD ANGRY?

HE WENT HENCE BUT NOW; AND CERTAINLY IN STRANGE UNQUIETNESS.

CAN HE BE ANGRY? I HAVE SEEN THE CANNON WHEN IT HATH BLOWN HIS RANKS INTO THE AIR, AND LIKE THE DEVIL FROM HIS VERY ARM PUFFED HIS OWN BROTHER. AND CAN HE BE ANGRY? SOMETHING OF MOMENT THEN. I WILL GO MEET HIM. THERE'S MATTER IN'T INDEED IF HE BE ANGRY.

I PRITHEE DO SO.

SOMETHING, SURE, OF STATE, EITHER FROM VENICE, OR SOME UNHATCHED PRACTICE MADE DEMONSTRABLE HERE IN CYPRUS TO HIM, HATH PUDDLED HIS CLEAR SPIRIT; AND IN SUCH CASES MEN'S NATURES WRANGLE WITH INFERIOR THINGS, THOUGH GREAT ONES ARE THEIR OBJECT. 'TIS EVEN SO.

FOR LET OUR FINGER ACHE, AND IT ENDUES OUR OTHER HEALTHFUL MEMBERS EVEN TO A SENSE OF PAIN.

NAY, WE MUST THINK MEN ARE NOT GODS, NOR OF THEM LOOK FOR SUCH OBSERVANCY AS FITS THE BRIDAL.

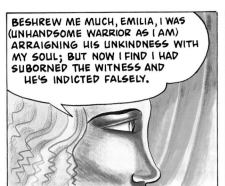

BESHREW ME MUCH, EMILIA, I WAS (UNHANDSOME WARRIOR AS I AM) ARRAIGNING HIS UNKINDNESS WITH MY SOUL; BUT NOW I FIND I HAD SUBORNED THE WITNESS AND HE'S INDICTED FALSELY.

PRAY HEAVEN IT BE STATE MATTERS, AS YOU THINK, AND NO CONCEPTION NOR NO JEALOUS TOY CONCERNING YOU.

ALAS THE DAY, I NEVER GAVE HIM CAUSE.

BUT JEALOUS SOULS WILL NOT BE ANSWERED SO; THEY ARE NOT EVER JEALOUS FOR THE CAUSE, BUT JEALOUS FOR THEY'RE JEALOUS. IT IS A MONSTER BEGOT UPON ITSELF, BORN ON ITSELF.

HEAVEN KEEP THAT MONSTER FROM OTHELLO'S MIND.

LADY, AMEN!

I WILL GO SEEK HIM. CASSIO, WALK HERE ABOUT. IF I DO FIND HIM FIT, I'LL MOVE YOUR SUIT, AND SEEK TO EFFECT IT TO MY UTTERMOST.

I HUMBLY THANK YOUR LADYSHIP.

ENTER BIANCA

WHAT MAKE YOU FROM HOME? HOW IS IT WITH YOU, MY MOST FAIR BIANCA? I'FAITH, SWEET LOVE, I WAS COMING TO YOUR HOUSE.

AND I WAS GOING TO YOUR LODGING, CASSIO.

'SAVE YOU, FRIEND CASSIO.

WHAT! KEEP A WEEK AWAY? SEVEN DAYS AND NIGHTS? EIGHT SCORE EIGHT HOURS? AND LOVERS' ABSENT HOURS MORE TEDIOUS THAN THE DIAL EIGHT SCORE TIMES!

O, WEARY RECKONING!

PARDON ME, BIANCA. I HAVE THIS WHILE WITH LEADEN THOUGHTS BEEN PRESSED: BUT I SHALL IN A MORE CONTINUATE TIME STRIKE OFF THIS SCORE OF ABSENCE.

SWEET BIANCA, TAKE ME THIS. WORK OUT.

O CASSIO, WHENCE CAME THIS?

THIS IS SOME TOKEN FROM A NEWER FRIEND. TO THE FELT ABSENCE NOW I FEEL A CAUSE. IS'T COME TO THIS? WELL, WELL.

GO TO, WOMAN!

THROW YOUR VILE GUESSES IN THE DEVIL'S TEETH FROM WHENCE YOU HAVE THEM. YOU ARE JEALOUS NOW THAT THIS IS FROM SOME MISTRESS — SOME REMEMBRANCE. NO, BY MY FAITH, BIANCA!

WHY, WHOSE IS IT?

I KNOW NOT, SWEET. I FOUND IT IN MY CHAMBER. I LIKE THE WORK WELL. ERE IT BE DEMANDED — AS LIKE ENOUGH IT WILL — I'D HAVE IT COPIED. TAKE IT AND DO'T. AND LEAVE ME FOR THIS TIME.

LEAVE YOU? WHEREFORE?

I DO ATTEND HERE ON THE GENERAL, AND THINK IT NO ADDITION, NOR MY WISH, TO HAVE HIM SEE ME WOMANED.

WHY, I PRAY YOU?

NOT THAT I LOVE YOU NOT.

BUT THAT YOU DO NOT LOVE ME. I PRAY YOU, BRING ME ON THE WAY A LITTLE, AND SAY IF I SHALL SEE YOU SOON AT NIGHT.

'TIS BUT A LITTLE WAY THAT I CAN BRING YOU, FOR I ATTEND HERE: BUT I'LL SEE YOU SOON.

'TIS VERY GOOD! I MUST BE CIRCUMSTANCED.

WILL YOU THINK SO?

THINK SO, IAGO?

WHAT, TO KISS IN PRIVATE?

AN UNAUTHORIZED KISS.

OR TO BE NAKED WITH HER FRIEND IN BED AN HOUR OR MORE, NOT MEANING ANY HARM?

NAKED IN BED, IAGO, AND NOT MEAN HARM? IT IS HYPOCRISY AGAINST THE DEVIL. THEY THAT MEAN VIRTUOUSLY, AND YET DO SO, THE DEVIL THEIR VIRTUE TEMPTS, AND THEY TEMPT HEAVEN.

IF THEY DO NOTHING, 'TIS A VENIAL SLIP. BUT IF I GIVE MY WIFE A HANDKERCHIEF—

WHAT THEN?

WHY, THEN, 'TIS HERS, MY LORD, AND BEING HERS, SHE MAY, I THINK, BESTOW'T ON ANY MAN.

SHE IS PROTECTRESS OF HER HONOUR TOO. MAY SHE GIVE THAT?

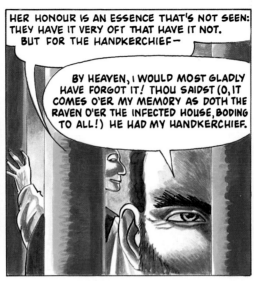

HER HONOUR IS AN ESSENCE THAT'S NOT SEEN: THEY HAVE IT VERY OFT THAT HAVE IT NOT. BUT FOR THE HANDKERCHIEF—

BY HEAVEN, I WOULD MOST GLADLY HAVE FORGOT IT! THOU SAIDST (O, IT COMES O'ER MY MEMORY AS DOTH THE RAVEN O'ER THE INFECTED HOUSE, BODING TO ALL!) HE HAD MY HANDKERCHIEF.

AY, WHAT OF THAT?

THAT'S NOT SO GOOD NOW.

WHAT IF I HAD SAID I HAD SEEN HIM DO YOU WRONG? OR HEARD HIM SAY —AS KNAVES BE SUCH ABROAD WHO, HAVING BY THEIR OWN IMPORTUNATE SUIT, OR VOLUNTARY DOTAGE OF SOME MISTRESS, CONVINCED OR SUPPLIED THEM, CANNOT CHOSE BUT THEY MUST BLAB—

HATH HE SAID ANYTHING?

HE HATH, MY LORD; BUT BE YOU WELL ASSURED, NO MORE THAN HE'LL UNSWEAR.

WHAT HATH HE SAID?

FAITH, THAT HE DID—I KNOW NOT WHAT HE DID.

WHAT? WHAT?

LIE.

WITH HER?

WITH HER, ON HER, WHAT YOU WILL.

LIE WITH HER? LIE ON HER?

WE SAY "LIE ON HER" WHEN THEY BELIE HER.

LIE WITH HER! ZOUNDS, THAT'S FULSOME!

HANDKERCHIEF - CONFESSIONS - HANDKERCHIEF!

TO CONFESS AND BE HANGED FOR HIS LABOUR. FIRST TO BE HANGED AND THEN TO CONFESS! I TREMBLE AT IT.

NATURE WOULD NOT INVEST HERSELF IN SUCH SHADOWING PASSION WITHOUT SOME INSTRUCTION.

IT IS NOT WORDS THAT SHAKES ME THUS!

PISH!

NOSES, EARS, AND LIPS! IS'T POSSIBLE? CONFESS? HANDKERCHIEF? O DEVIL!

WORK ON, MY MEDICINE, WORK.

THUS CREDULOUS FOOLS ARE CAUGHT; AND MANY WORTHY AND CHASTE DAMES EVEN THUS, ALL GUILTLESS, MEET REPROACH.

WHAT HO, MY LORD! MY LORD, I SAY! OTHELLO!

HOW NOW, CASSIO!

WHAT'S THE MATTER?

MY LORD IS FALLEN INTO AN EPILEPSY. THIS IS HIS SECOND FIT: HE HAD ONE YESTERDAY.

RUB HIM ABOUT THE TEMPLES.

NO, FORBEAR. THE LETHARGY MUST HAVE HIS QUIET COURSE. IF NOT, HE FOAMS AT MOUTH, AND BY AND BY BREAKS OUT TO SAVAGE MADNESS.

LOOK, HE STIRS.

DO YOU WITHDRAW YOURSELF A LITTLE WHILE. HE WILL RECOVER STRAIGHT. WHEN HE IS GONE, I WOULD ON GREAT OCCASION SPEAK WITH YOU.

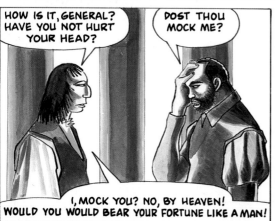

HOW IS IT, GENERAL? HAVE YOU NOT HURT YOUR HEAD?

DOST THOU MOCK ME?

I, MOCK YOU? NO, BY HEAVEN! WOULD YOU WOULD BEAR YOUR FORTUNE LIKE A MAN!

A HORNÈD MAN'S A MONSTER AND A BEAST.

THERE'S MANY A BEAST THEN IN A POPULOUS CITY. AND MANY A CIVIL MONSTER.

DID HE CONFESS IT?

GOOD SIR, BE A MAN. THINK EVERY BEARDED FELLOW THAT'S BUT YOKED MAY DRAW WITH YOU. THERE'S MILLIONS NOW ALIVE THAT NIGHTLY LIE IN THOSE UNPROPER BEDS WHICH THEY DARE SWEAR PECULIAR. YOUR CASE IS BETTER.

O, 'TIS THE SPITE OF HELL, THE FIEND'S ARCH-MOCK, TO LIP A WANTON IN A SECURE COUCH, AND TO SUPPOSE HER CHASTE! NO, LET ME KNOW; AND KNOWING WHAT I AM, I KNOW WHAT SHALL BE.

O, THOU ART WISE, 'TIS CERTAIN.

STAND YOU AWHILE APART; CONFINE YOURSELF BUT IN A PATIENT LIST. WHILST YOU WERE HERE, O'ERWHELMÈD WITH YOUR GRIEF— A PASSION MOST UNSUITING SUCH A MAN—CASSIO CAME HITHER. I SHIFTED HIM AWAY AND LAID GOOD 'SCUSE UPON YOUR ECSTASY; BADE HIM ANON RETURN AND HERE SPEAK WITH ME, THE WHICH HE PROMISED.

DO BUT ENCAVE YOURSELF, AND MARK THE FLEERS, THE GIBES AND NOTABLE SCORNS THAT DWELL IN EVERY REGION OF HIS FACE.

FOR I WILL MAKE HIM TELL THE TALE ANEW — WHERE, HOW, HOW OFT, HOW LONG, AGO, AND WHEN HE HATH, AND IS AGAIN, TO COPE YOUR WIFE. I SAY, BUT MARK HIS GESTURES.

MARRY, PATIENCE! OR I SHALL SAY YOU'RE ALL IN ALL IN SPLEEN AND NOTHING OF A MAN.

DOST THOU HEAR, IAGO? I WILL BE FOUND MOST CUNNING IN MY PATIENCE, BUT — DOST THOU HEAR? — MOST BLOODY.

THAT'S NOT AMISS, BUT YET KEEP TIME IN ALL. WILL YOU WITHDRAW?

NOW WILL I QUESTION CASSIO OF BIANCA, A HOUSEWIFE, THAT BY SELLING HER DESIRES BUYS HERSELF BREAD AND CLOTHES. IT IS A CREATURE THAT DOTES ON CASSIO — AS 'TIS THE STRUMPET'S PLAGUE TO BEGUILE MANY AND BE BEGUILED BY ONE. HE, WHEN HE HEARS OF HER, CANNOT REFRAIN FROM THE EXCESS OF LAUGHTER.

HERE HE COMES.

AS HE SHALL SMILE, OTHELLO SHALL GO MAD; AND HIS UNBOOKISH JEALOUSY MUST CONSTRUE POOR CASSIO'S SMILES, GESTURES, AND LIGHT BEHAVIOUR QUITE IN THE WRONG.

HOW DO YOU NOW, LIEUTENANT?

THE WORSER THAT YOU GIVE ME THE ADDITION WHOSE WANT EVEN KILLS ME.

PLY DESDEMONA WELL AND YOU ARE SURE ON'T.

NOW IF THIS SUIT LAY IN BIANCA'S POWER, HOW QUICKLY SHOULD YOU SPEED!

ALAS, POOR CAITIFF!

LOOK HOW HE LAUGHS ALREADY!

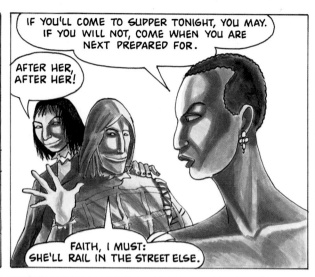

NAY, THAT'S NOT YOUR WAY.

HANG HER! I DO BUT SAY WHAT SHE IS: SO DELICATE WITH HER NEEDLE, AN ADMIRABLE MUSICIAN!

O, SHE WILL SING THE SAVAGENESS OUT OF A BEAR! OF SO HIGH AND PLENTEOUS WIT AND INVENTION!

SHE'S THE WORSE FOR ALL THIS.

O, A THOUSAND, A THOUSAND TIMES! — AND THEN OF SO GENTLE A CONDITION.

AY, TOO GENTLE.

NAY, THAT'S CERTAIN — BUT YET THE PITY OF IT, IAGO! O, IAGO, THE PITY OF IT, IAGO!

IF YOU ARE SO FOND OVER HER INIQUITY, GIVE HER PATENT TO OFFEND, FOR IF IT TOUCH NOT YOU, IT COMES NEAR NOBODY.

I WILL CHOP HER INTO MESSES! CUCKOLD ME!

O, 'TIS FOUL IN HER!

WITH MINE OFFICER!

THAT'S FOULER.

GET ME SOME POISON, IAGO, THIS NIGHT. I'LL NOT EXPOSTULATE WITH HER, LEST HER BODY AND BEAUTY UNPROVIDE MY MIND AGAIN — THIS NIGHT, IAGO.

DO IT NOT WITH POISON — STRANGLE HER IN HER BED, EVEN THE BED SHE HATH CONTAMINATED.

GOOD, GOOD! THE JUSTICE OF IT PLEASES; VERY GOOD!

AND FOR CASSIO, LET ME BE HIS UNDERTAKER. YOU SHALL HEAR MORE BY MIDNIGHT.

EXCELLENT GOOD!

WHAT TRUMPET IS THAT SAME?

I WARRANT, SOMETHING FROM VENICE.

ENTER LODOVICO, DESDEMONA AND ATTENDANTS.

'TIS LODOVICO, COME FROM THE DUKE, AND SEE YOUR WIFE IS WITH HIM.

GOD SAVE THE WORTHY GENERAL!

WITH ALL MY HEART, SIR.

THE DUKE AND SENATORS OF VENICE GREET YOU.

I KISS THE INSTRUMENT OF THEIR PLEASURES.

AND WHAT'S THE NEWS, GOOD COUSIN LODOVICO?

I AM VERY GLAD TO SEE YOU, SIGNOR: WELCOME TO CYPRUS.

I THANK YOU. HOW DOES LIEUTENANT CASSIO?

LIVES, SIR.

COUSIN, THERE'S FALLEN BETWEEN HIM AND MY LORD AN UNKIND BREACH; BUT YOU SHALL MAKE ALL WELL.

ARE YOU SURE OF THAT?

MY LORD?

"THIS FAIL YOU NOT TO DO, AS YOU WILL"—

HE DID NOT CALL: HE'S BUSY IN THE PAPER. IS THERE DIVISION 'TWIXT MY LORD AND CASSIO?

A MOST UNHAPPY ONE; I WOULD DO MUCH T'ATONE THEM, FOR THE LOVE I BEAR TO CASSIO.

FIRE AND BRIMSTONE!

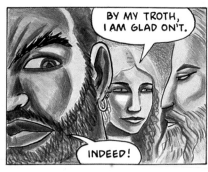

TRULY AN OBEDIENT LADY. I DO BESEECH YOUR LORDSHIP CALL HER BACK.

MISTRESS!

MY LORD?

WHAT WOULD YOU WITH HER, SIR?

WHO? I, MY LORD?

AY, YOU DID WISH THAT I WOULD MAKE HER TURN. SIR, SHE CAN TURN, AND TURN, AND YET GO ON, AND TURN AGAIN.

AND SHE CAN WEEP, SIR, WEEP. AND SHE'S OBEDIENT; AS YOU SAY, OBEDIENT, VERY OBEDIENT.
—PROCEED YOU IN YOUR TEARS—
CONCERNING THIS, SIR—
O, WELL-PAINTED PASSION!—
I AM COMMANDED HOME.

GET YOU AWAY! I'LL SEND FOR YOU ANON.

SIR, I OBEY THE MANDATE AND WILL RETURN TO VENICE.
—HENCE, AVAUNT!

CASSIO SHALL HAVE MY PLACE.

AND, SIR, TONIGHT I DO ENTREAT THAT WE MAY SUP TOGETHER.

YOU ARE WELCOME, SIR, TO CYPRUS.

GOATS AND MONKEYS!

IS THIS THE NOBLE MOOR, WHOM OUR FULL SENATE CALL ALL-IN-ALL SUFFICIENT? IS THIS THE NATURE WHOM PASSION COULD NOT SHAKE? WHOSE SOLID VIRTUE THE SHOT OF ACCIDENT NOR DART OF CHANCE COULD NEITHER GRAZE NOR PIERCE?

HE IS MUCH CHANGED.

ARE HIS WITS SAFE? IS HE NOT LIGHT OF BRAIN?

HE'S THAT HE IS: I MAY NOT BREATHE MY CENSURE WHAT HE MIGHT BE. IF WHAT HE MIGHT HE IS NOT, I WOULD TO HEAVEN HE WERE.

WHAT! STRIKE HIS WIFE?

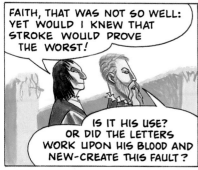

FAITH, THAT WAS NOT SO WELL: YET WOULD I KNEW THAT STROKE WOULD PROVE THE WORST!

IS IT HIS USE? OR DID THE LETTERS WORK UPON HIS BLOOD AND NEW-CREATE THIS FAULT?

ALAS, ALAS! IT IS NOT HONESTY IN ME TO SPEAK WHAT I HAVE SEEN AND KNOWN. YOU SHALL OBSERVE HIM, AND HIS OWN COURSES WILL DENOTE HIM SO, THAT I MAY SAVE MY SPEECH. DO BUT GO AFTER, AND MARK HOW HE CONTINUES.

I AM SORRY THAT I AM DECEIVED IN HIM.

ARE YOU NOT A STRUMPET?

NO, AS I AM A CHRISTIAN. IF TO PRESERVE THIS VESSEL FOR MY LORD FROM ANY OTHER FOUL UNLAWFUL TOUCH BE NOT TO BE A STRUMPET, I AM NONE.

WHAT! NOT A WHORE?

NO, AS I SHALL BE SAVED.

IS'T POSSIBLE?

O, HEAVEN FORGIVE US!

I CRY YOU MERCY THEN: I TOOK YOU FOR THAT CUNNING WHORE OF VENICE THAT MARRIED WITH OTHELLO.

YOU, MISTRESS, THAT HAVE THE OFFICE OPPOSITE TO SAINT PETER AND KEEP THE GATE OF HELL!

YOU, YOU, AY, YOU! WE HAVE DONE OUR COURSE. THERE'S MONEY FOR YOUR PAINS.

I PRAY YOU TURN THE KEY AND KEEP YOUR COUNSEL.

ALAS, WHAT DOES THIS GENTLEMAN CONCEIVE? HOW DO YOU, MADAM? HOW DO YOU, MY GOOD LADY?

FAITH, HALF ASLEEP.

GOOD MADAM, WHAT'S THE MATTER WITH MY LORD?

WITH WHO?

WHY, WITH MY LORD, MADAM.

WHO IS THY LORD?

HE THAT IS YOURS, SWEET LADY.

I HAVE NONE. DO NOT TALK TO ME, EMILIA: I CANNOT WEEP, NOR ANSWERS HAVE I NONE BUT WHAT SHOULD GO BY WATER. PRITHEE TONIGHT LAY ON MY BED MY WEDDING SHEETS. REMEMBER. AND CALL THY HUSBAND HITHER.

HERE'S A CHANGE INDEED.

'TIS MEET I SHOULD BE USED SO, VERY MEET. HOW HAVE I BEEN BEHAVED, THAT HE MIGHT STICK THE SMALLEST OPINION ON MY LEAST MISUSE?

WHAT IS YOUR PLEASURE, MADAM? HOW IS'T WITH YOU?

I CANNOT TELL: THOSE THAT DO TEACH YOUNG BABES DO IT WITH GENTLE MEANS AND EASY TASKS: HE MIGHT HAVE CHID ME SO, FOR, IN GOOD FAITH, I AM A CHILD TO CHIDING.

WHAT IS THE MATTER, LADY?

ALAS, IAGO, MY LORD HATH SO BEWHORED HER, THROWN SUCH DESPITE AND HEAVY TERMS UPON HER AS TRUE HEART CANNOT BEAR!

AM I THAT NAME, IAGO?

WHAT NAME, FAIR LADY?

SUCH AS SHE SAID MY LORD DID SAY I WAS.

HE CALLED HER WHORE: A BEGGAR IN HIS DRINK COULD NOT HAVE LAID SUCH TERMS UPON HIS CALLET.

WHY DID HE SO?

I DO NOT KNOW: I AM SURE I AM NONE SUCH.

DO NOT WEEP, DO NOT WEEP. ALAS THE DAY!

HATH SHE FORSOOK SO MANY NOBLE MATCHES, HER FATHER, AND HER COUNTRY, ALL HER FRIENDS, TO BE CALLED WHORE? WOULD IT NOT MAKE ONE WEEP?

IT IS MY WRETCHED FORTUNE.

BESHREW HIM FOR'T! HOW COMES THIS TRICK UPON HIM?

NAY, HEAVEN DOTH KNOW.

I WILL BE HANGED IF SOME ETERNAL VILLAIN, SOME BUSY AND INSINUATING ROGUE, SOME COGGING, COZENING SLAVE, TO GET SOME OFFICE, HAVE NOT DEVISED THIS SLANDER; I'LL BE HANGED ELSE.

FIE, THERE IS NO SUCH MAN! IT IS IMPOSSIBLE.

IF ANY SUCH THERE BE, HEAVEN PARDON HIM.

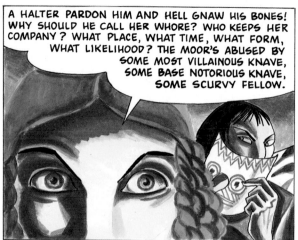

A HALTER PARDON HIM AND HELL GNAW HIS BONES! WHY SHOULD HE CALL HER WHORE? WHO KEEPS HER COMPANY? WHAT PLACE, WHAT TIME, WHAT FORM, WHAT LIKELIHOOD? THE MOOR'S ABUSED BY SOME MOST VILLAINOUS KNAVE, SOME BASE NOTORIOUS KNAVE, SOME SCURVY FELLOW.

O HEAVEN, THAT SUCH COMPANIONS THOU'DST UNFOLD, AND PUT IN EVERY HONEST HAND A WHIP TO LASH THE RASCALS NAKED THROUGH THE WORLD, EVEN FROM THE EAST TO TH'WEST.

SPEAK WITHIN-DOOR!

O FIE UPON THEM! SOME SUCH SQUIRE HE WAS THAT TURNED YOUR WIT THE SEAMY SIDE WITHOUT AND MADE YOU TO SUSPECT ME WITH THE MOOR.

YOU ARE A FOOL, GO TO.

O GOOD IAGO, WHAT SHALL I DO TO WIN MY LORD AGAIN? GOOD FRIEND, GO TO HIM; FOR, BY THIS LIGHT OF HEAVEN, I KNOW NOT HOW I LOST HIM.

HERE I KNEEL: IF E'ER MY WILL DID TRESPASS 'GAINST HIS LOVE, EITHER IN DISCOURSE OF THOUGHT OR ACTUAL DEED; OR THAT MINE EYES, MINE EARS OR ANY SENSE DELIGHTED THEM IN ANY OTHER FORM; OR THAT I DO NOT YET, AND EVER DID, AND EVER WILL — THOUGH HE DO SHAKE ME OFF TO BEGGARLY DIVORCEMENT — LOVE HIM DEARLY, COMFORT FORSWEAR ME!

UNKINDNESS MAY DO MUCH, AND HIS UNKINDNESS MAY DEFEAT MY LIFE, BUT NEVER TAINT MY LOVE. I CANNOT SAY "WHORE": IT DOES ABHOR ME NOW I SPEAK THE WORD; TO DO THE ACT THAT MIGHT THE ADDITION EARN — NOT THE WORLD'S MASS OF VANITY COULD MAKE ME.

I PRAY YOU, BE CONTENT: 'TIS BUT HIS HUMOUR; THE BUSINESS OF THE STATE DOES HIM OFFENCE, AND HE DOES CHIDE WITH YOU.

IF 'TWERE NO OTHER—

IT IS BUT SO, I WARRANT.

HARK HOW THESE INSTRUMENTS SUMMON TO SUPPER! THE MESSENGERS OF VENICE STAY THE MEAT.

GO IN, AND WEEP NOT; ALL THINGS SHALL BE WELL.

HOW NOW, RODERIGO?

I DO NOT FIND THAT THOU DEAL'ST JUSTLY WITH ME.

WHAT IN THE CONTRARY?

EVERY DAY THOU DAFF'ST ME WITH SOME DEVICE, IAGO, AND RATHER, AS IT SEEMS TO ME NOW, KEEP'ST FROM ME ALL CONVENIENCY, THAN SUPPLIEST ME WITH THE LEAST ADVANTAGE OF HOPE. I WILL INDEED NO LONGER ENDURE IT. NOR AM I YET PERSUADED TO PUT UP IN PEACE WHAT ALREADY I HAVE FOOLISHLY SUFFERED.

WILL YOU HEAR ME, RODERIGO?

FAITH, I HAVE HEARD TOO MUCH; FOR YOUR WORDS AND PERFORMANCES ARE NO KIN TOGETHER.

YOU CHARGE ME MOST UNJUSTLY.

WITH NAUGHT BUT TRUTH. I HAVE WASTED MYSELF OUT OF MY MEANS. THE JEWELS YOU HAVE HAD FROM ME TO DELIVER TO DESDEMONA WOULD HALF HAVE CORRUPTED A VOTARIST. YOU HAVE TOLD ME SHE HATH RECEIVED THEM, AND RETURNED ME EXPECTATIONS AND COMFORTS OF SUDDEN RESPECT AND ACQUAINTANCE — BUT I FIND NONE.

WELL, GO TO; VERY WELL.

VERY WELL? GO TO? I CANNOT GO TO, MAN, NOR 'TIS NOT VERY WELL. NAY, I THINK IT IS SCURVY, AND BEGIN TO FIND MYSELF FOPPED IN IT.

VERY WELL.

I TELL YOU, 'TIS NOT VERY WELL. I WILL MAKE MYSELF KNOWN TO DESDEMONA.

IF SHE WILL RETURN ME MY JEWELS, I WILL GIVE OVER MY SUIT AND REPENT MY UNLAWFUL SOLICITATION. –IF NOT, ASSURE YOURSELF I WILL SEEK SATISFACTION OF YOU.

YOU HAVE SAID NOW.

AY, AND SAID NOTHING BUT WHAT I PROTEST INTENDMENT OF DOING.

WHY, NOW I SEE THERE'S METTLE IN THEE; AND EVEN FROM THIS INSTANT DO BUILD ON THEE A BETTER OPINION THAN EVER BEFORE. GIVE ME THY HAND, RODERIGO. THOU HAST TAKEN AGAINST ME A MOST JUST EXCEPTION; BUT YET I PROTEST I HAVE DEALT MOST DIRECTLY IN THY AFFAIR.

IT HATH NOT APPEARED.

I GRANT INDEED IT HATH NOT APPEARED; AND YOUR SUSPICION IS NOT WITHOUT WIT AND JUDGEMENT. BUT, RODERIGO, IF THOU HAST THAT IN THEE INDEED– WHICH I HAVE GREATER REASON TO BELIEVE NOW THAN EVER (I MEAN PURPOSE, COURAGE AND VALOUR)– THIS NIGHT SHOW IT!

IF THOU THE NEXT NIGHT FOLLOWING ENJOY NOT DESDEMONA, TAKE ME FROM THIS WORLD WITH TREACHERY, AND DEVISE ENGINES FOR MY LIFE.

WELL, WHAT IS IT? IS IT WITHIN REASON AND COMPASS?

SIR, THERE IS ESPECIAL COMMISSION COME FROM VENICE TO DEPUTE CASSIO IN OTHELLO'S PLACE.

IS THAT TRUE? WHY, THEN OTHELLO AND DESDEMONA RETURN AGAIN TO VENICE.

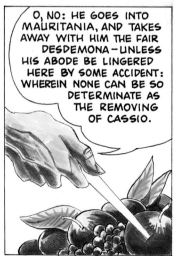

O, NO: HE GOES INTO MAURITANIA, AND TAKES AWAY WITH HIM THE FAIR DESDEMONA–UNLESS HIS ABODE BE LINGERED HERE BY SOME ACCIDENT: WHEREIN NONE CAN BE SO DETERMINATE AS THE REMOVING OF CASSIO.

HOW DO YOU MEAN, "REMOVING" OF HIM?

WHY, BY MAKING HIM UNCAPABLE OF OTHELLO'S PLACE– KNOCKING OUT HIS BRAINS.

AND THAT YOU WOULD HAVE ME TO DO?

AY, IF YOU DARE DO YOURSELF A PROFIT AND A RIGHT. HE SUPS TONIGHT WITH A HARLOTRY; AND THITHER WILL I GO TO HIM. HE KNOWS NOT YET OF HIS HONOURABLE FORTUNE.

IF YOU WILL WATCH HIS GOING THENCE–WHICH I WILL FASHION TO FALL OUT BETWEEN TWELVE AND ONE– YOU MAY TAKE HIM AT YOUR PLEASURE.

I WILL BE NEAR TO SECOND YOUR ATTEMPT, AND HE SHALL FALL BETWEEN US.

COME, STAND NOT AMAZED AT IT, BUT GO ALONG WITH ME.

I WILL SHOW YOU SUCH A NECESSITY IN HIS DEATH THAT YOU SHALL THINK YOURSELF BOUND TO PUT IT ON HIM.

IT IS NOW HIGH SUPPER-TIME, AND THE NIGHT GROWS TO WASTE. —ABOUT IT!

I WILL HEAR FURTHER REASON FOR THIS.

AND YOU SHALL BE SATISFIED.

ACT IV, SCENE III

I DO BESEECH YOU, SIR, TROUBLE YOURSELF NO FURTHER.

O, PARDON ME: 'TWILL DO ME GOOD TO WALK.

MADAM, GOOD NIGHT. I HUMBLY THANK YOUR LADYSHIP.

YOUR HONOUR IS MOST WELCOME.

WILL YOU WALK, SIR?

O, DESDEMONA!

MY LORD?

GET YOU TO BED ON TH'INSTANT. I WILL BE RETURNED FORTHWITH. DISMISS YOUR ATTENDANT THERE. LOOK'T BE DONE.

I WILL, MY LORD.

HOW GOES IT NOW? HE LOOKS GENTLER THAN HE DID.

HE SAYS HE WILL RETURN INCONTINENT. HE HATH COMMANDED ME TO GO TO BED, AND BADE ME TO DISMISS YOU.

DISMISS ME?

IT WAS HIS BIDDING: THEREFORE, GOOD EMILIA, GIVE ME MY NIGHTLY WEARING, AND ADIEU. WE MUST NOT NOW DISPLEASE HIM.

I WOULD YOU HAD NEVER SEEN HIM.

SO WOULD NOT I: MY LOVE DOTH SO APPROVE HIM THAT EVEN HIS STUBBORNESS, HIS CHECKS, HIS FROWNS —PRITHEE, UNPIN ME— HAVE GRACE AND FAVOUR IN THEM.

I HAVE LAID THOSE SHEETS YOU BADE ME ON THE BED.

ALL'S ONE. GOOD FAITH, HOW FOOLISH ARE OUR MINDS! IF I DO DIE BEFORE THEE, PRITHEE SHROUD ME IN ONE OF THOSE SAME SHEETS.

COME, COME, YOU TALK.

MY MOTHER HAD A MAID CALLED BARBARY. SHE WAS IN LOVE: AND HE SHE LOVED PROVED MAD AND DID FORSAKE HER. SHE HAD A SONG OF 'WILLOW'— AN OLD THING 'TWAS; BUT IT EXPRESSED HER FORTUNE, AND SHE DIED SINGING IT.

THAT SONG TONIGHT WILL NOT GO FROM MY MIND: I HAVE MUCH TO DO BUT TO GO HANG MY HEAD ALL AT ONE SIDE, AND SING IT LIKE POOR BARBARY. —PRITHEE DISPATCH.

SHALL I GO FETCH YOUR NIGHT-GOWN?

NO, UNPIN ME HERE. THIS LODOVICO IS A PROPER MAN.

A VERY HANDSOME MAN.

I KNOW A LADY IN VENICE WOULD HAVE WALKED BAREFOOT TO PALESTINE FOR A TOUCH OF HIS NETHER LIP.

THE POOR SOUL SAT SIGHING BY A SYCAMORE TREE, SING ALL A GREEN WILLOW; HER HAND ON HER BOSOM, HER HEAD ON HER KNEE, SING WILLOW, WILLOW, WILLOW; THE FRESH STREAMS RAN BY HER AND MURMURED HER MOANS; SING WILLOW, WILLOW, WILLOW; HER SALT TEARS FELL FROM HER AND SOFTENED THE STONES—

LAY BY THESE.

SING WILLOW, WILLOW, WILLOW—

PRITHEE HIE THEE; HE'LL COME ANON.

SING ALL A GREEN WILLOW MUST BE MY GARLAND. LET NOBODY BLAME HIM; HIS SCORN I APPROVE—

NAY, THAT'S NOT NEXT. HARK, WHO IS'T THAT KNOCKS?

IT'S THE WIND.

I CALLED MY LOVE FALSE LOVE, BUT WHAT SAID HE THEN? SING WILLOW, WILLOW, WILLOW: IF I COURT MOE WOMEN, YOU'LL COUCH WITH MOE MEN.

SO GET THEE GONE; GOOD NIGHT. MINE EYES DO ITCH: DOES THAT BODE WEEPING?

'TIS NEITHER HERE NOR THERE.

I HAVE HEARD IT SAID SO. O, THESE MEN, THESE MEN! DOST THOU IN CONSCIENCE THINK— TELL ME, EMILIA—THAT THERE BE WOMEN DO ABUSE THEIR HUSBANDS IN SUCH GROSS KIND?

THERE BE SOME SUCH, NO QUESTION.

WOULDST THOU DO SUCH A DEED FOR ALL THE WORLD?

WHY, WOULD NOT YOU?

NO, BY THIS HEAVENLY LIGHT.

NOR I NEITHER BY THIS HEAVENLY LIGHT: I MIGHT DO'T AS WELL I'TH' DARK.

WOULDST THOU DO SUCH A THING FOR ALL THE WORLD?

THE WORLD'S A HUGE THING: IT IS A GREAT PRICE FOR A SMALL VICE.

IN TROTH, I THINK THOU WOULDST NOT.

IN TROTH I THINK I SHOULD, AND UNDO'T WHEN I HAD DONE. MARRY, I WOULD NOT DO SUCH A THING FOR A JOINT-RING, NOR FOR MEASURES OF LAWN, NOR FOR GOWNS, PETTICOATS, NOR CAPS, NOR ANY PETTY EXHIBITION.

BUT FOR ALL THE WHOLE WORLD! UD'S PITY, WHO WOULD NOT MAKE HER HUSBAND A CUCKOLD, TO MAKE HIM A MONARCH? I SHOULD VENTURE PURGATORY FOR'T.

BESHREW ME, IF I WOULD DO SUCH A WRONG FOR THE WHOLE WORLD!

WHY, THE WRONG IS BUT A WRONG I'TH' WORLD; AND HAVING THE WORLD FOR YOUR LABOUR, 'TIS A WRONG IN YOUR OWN WORLD, AND YOU MIGHT QUICKLY MAKE IT RIGHT.

I DO NOT THINK THERE IS ANY SUCH WOMAN.

YES, A DOZEN: AND AS MANY TO TH' VANTAGE AS WOULD STORE THE WORLD THEY PLAYED FOR.

BUT I DO THINK IT IS THEIR HUSBANDS' FAULTS
IF WIVES DO FALL. SAY THAT THEY SLACK THEIR DUTIES,
AND POUR OUR TREASURES INTO FOREIGN LAPS;
OR ELSE BREAK OUT IN PEEVISH JEALOUSIES,
THROWING RESTRAINT UPON US; OR SAY THEY STRIKE US,
OR SCANT OUR FORMER HAVING IN DESPITE—
WHY, WE HAVE GALLS, AND THOUGH WE HAVE SOME GRACE,
    YET HAVE WE SOME REVENGE.

LET HUSBANDS KNOW THEIR WIVES HAVE SENSE LIKE THEM:
THEY SEE, AND SMELL, AND HAVE THEIR PALATES
BOTH FOR SWEET AND SOUR, AS HUSBANDS HAVE.
WHAT IS IT THAT THEY DO, WHEN THEY CHANGE US
FOR OTHERS? IS IT SPORT? I THINK IT IS.
AND DOTH AFFECTION BREED IT?
    I THINK IT DOTH.

IS'T FRAILTY THAT THUS ERRS? IT IS SO TOO.
AND HAVE NOT WE AFFECTIONS, DESIRES FOR SPORT,
AND FRAILTY, AS MEN HAVE? THEN LET THEM USE
US WELL: ELSE LET THEM KNOW THE ILLS WE DO,
THEIR ILLS INSTRUCT US SO.

GOOD NIGHT, GOOD NIGHT.

GOD ME SUCH USES SEND,
NOT TO PICK BAD FROM BAD,
BUT BY BAD MEND!

IF CASSIO DO REMAIN HE HATH A DAILY BEAUTY IN HIS LIFE THAT MAKES ME UGLY: AND BESIDES, THE MOOR MAY UNFOLD ME TO HIM—

THERE STAND I IN MUCH PERIL. NO, HE MUST DIE.

BUT SOFT, I HEAR HIM COMING.

I KNOW HIS GAIT; 'TIS HE.

VILLAIN, THOU DIEST!

THAT THRUST HAD BEEN MINE ENEMY INDEED, BUT THAT MY COAT IS BETTER THAN THOU KNOW'ST.

I WILL MAKE PROOF OF THINE!

O, I AM SLAIN!

I AM MAIMED FOR EVER HELP, HO!

MURDER, MURDER!

THE VOICE OF CASSIO: IAGO KEEPS HIS WORD.

O, VILLAIN THAT I AM!

IT IS EVEN SO.

O, HELP, HO! LIGHT! A SURGEON!

'TIS HE! O BRAVE IAGO, HONEST AND JUST, THAT HAST SUCH NOBLE SENSE OF THY FRIEND'S WRONG, THOU TEACHEST ME!

MINION, YOUR DEAR LIES DEAD, AND YOUR UNBLEST FATE HIES.

STRUMPET, I COME!

FORTH OF MY HEART THOSE CHARMS, THINE EYES, ARE BLOTTED; THY BED, LUST-STAINED, SHALL WITH LUST'S BLOOD BE SPOTTED.

WHAT HO! NO WATCH? NO PASSAGE? MURDER! MURDER!

ENTER GRATIANO AND LODOVICO

'TIS SOME MISCHANCE: THE CRY IS VERY DIREFUL.

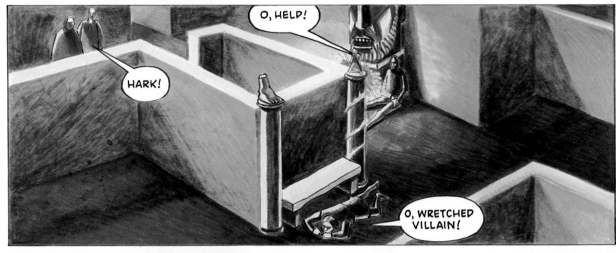
O, HELP!

HARK!

O, WRETCHED VILLAIN!

TWO OR THREE GROAN. 'TIS HEAVY NIGHT; THESE MAY BE COUNTERFEITS. LET'S THINK'T UNSAFE TO COME IN TO THE CRY WITHOUT MORE HELP.

NOBODY COME? THEN SHALL I BLEED TO DEATH.

HARK!

HERE'S ONE COMES IN HIS SHIRT, WITH LIGHT AND WEAPONS.

WHO'S THERE? WHOSE NOISE IS THIS THAT CRIES ON MURDER?

WHAT, LOOK YOU PALE?

O, BEAR HIM OUT O'TH'AIR.

STAY YOU, GOOD GENTLEMEN.

LOOK YOU PALE, MISTRESS?

DO YOU PERCEIVE THE GASTNESS OF HER EYE? NAY, IF YOU STARE, WE SHALL HEAR MORE ANON. BEHOLD HER WELL; I PRAY YOU LOOK UPON HER.

DO YOU SEE, GENTLEMEN?

NAY, GUILTINESS WILL SPEAK, THOUGH TONGUES WERE OUT OF USE.

'LAS WHAT'S THE MATTER? WHAT'S THE MATTER, HUSBAND?

CASSIO HATH HERE BEEN SET ON IN THE DARK BY RODERIGO AND FELLOWS THAT ARE 'SCAPED: HE'S ALMOST SLAIN, AND RODERIGO DEAD.

ALAS, GOOD GENTLEMAN! ALAS, GOOD CASSIO!

THIS IS THE FRUIT OF WHORING. PRITHEE, EMILIA, GO KNOW OF CASSIO WHERE HE SUPPED TONIGHT.

WHAT, DO YOU SHAKE AT THAT?

HE SUPPED AT MY HOUSE, BUT I THEREFORE SHAKE NOT.

O, DID HE SO? I CHARGE YOU GO WITH ME.

O, FIE UPON THEE, STRUMPET!

I AM NO STRUMPET, BUT OF LIFE AS HONEST AS YOU THAT THUS ABUSE ME.

AS I? FOH! FIE UPON THEE!

KIND GENTLEMEN, LET'S GO SEE POOR CASSIO DRESSED.

COME, MISTRESS, YOU MUST TELL'S ANOTHER TALE.

EMILIA, RUN YOU TO THE CITADEL, AND TELL MY LORD AND LADY WHAT HATH HAPPED. WILL YOU GO ON AFORE?

THIS IS THE NIGHT THAT EITHER MAKES ME, OR FORDOES ME QUITE.

IT IS THE CAUSE, IT IS THE CAUSE, MY SOUL; LET ME NOT NAME IT TO YOU, YOU CHASTE STARS: IT IS THE CAUSE. YET I'LL NOT SHED HER BLOOD, NOR SCAR THAT WHITER SKIN OF HERS THAN SNOW, AND SMOOTH AS MONUMENTAL ALABASTER:

YET SHE MUST DIE, ELSE SHE'LL BETRAY MORE MEN.

PUT OUT THE LIGHT, AND THEN PUT OUT THE LIGHT.

IF I QUENCH THEE, THOU FLAMING MINISTER, I CAN AGAIN THY FORMER LIGHT RESTORE, SHOULD I REPENT ME;

BUT ONCE PUT OUT THY LIGHT, THOU CUNNING'ST PATTERN OF EXCELLING NATURE, I KNOW NOT WHERE IS THAT PROMETHEAN HEAT THAT CAN THY LIGHT RELUME.

WHEN I HAVE PLUCKED THY ROSE, I CANNOT GIVE IT VITAL GROWTH AGAIN, IT NEEDS MUST WITHER.

I'LL SMELL IT ON THE TREE.

O BALMY BREATH, THAT DOTH ALMOST PERSUADE JUSTICE TO BREAK HER SWORD! ONE MORE, ONE MORE. BE THUS WHEN THOU ART DEAD AND I WILL KILL THEE AND LOVE THEE AFTER.

ONE MORE, AND THIS THE LAST.

SO SWEET WAS NE'ER SO FATAL. I MUST WEEP...BUT THEY ARE CRUEL TEARS: THIS SORROW'S HEAVENLY-IT STRIKES WHERE IT DOTH LOVE.

SHE WAKES.

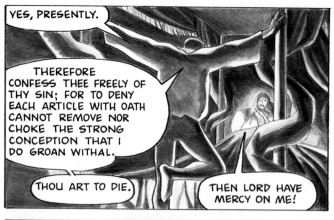

YES, PRESENTLY.

THEREFORE CONFESS THEE FREELY OF THY SIN; FOR TO DENY EACH ARTICLE WITH OATH CANNOT REMOVE NOR CHOKE THE STRONG CONCEPTION THAT I DO GROAN WITHAL.

THOU ART TO DIE.

THEN LORD HAVE MERCY ON ME!

I SAY, AMEN.

AND HAVE YOU MERCY TOO! I NEVER DID OFFEND YOU IN MY LIFE; NEVER LOVED CASSIO, BUT WITH SUCH GENERAL WARRANTY OF HEAVEN AS I MIGHT LOVE. I NEVER GAVE HIM TOKEN.

BY HEAVEN, I SAW MY HANDKERCHIEF IN'S HAND! O PERJURED WOMAN!

THOU DOST STONE MY HEART, AND MAK'ST ME CALL WHAT I INTEND TO DO A MURDER, WHICH I THOUGHT A SACRIFICE.

I SAW THE HANDKERCHIEF!

HE FOUND IT THEN. I NEVER GAVE IT HIM. SEND FOR HIM HITHER.

LET HIM CONFESS A TRUTH.

HE HATH CONFESSED.

WHAT, MY LORD?

THAT HE HATH USED THEE.

HOW? UNLAWFULLY?

AY.

HE WILL NOT SAY SO!

NO, HIS MOUTH IS STOPPED: HONEST IAGO HATH TA'EN ORDER FOR'T.

O, MY FEAR INTERPRETS! —WHAT, IS HE DEAD?

HAD ALL HIS HAIRS BEEN LIVES, MY GREAT REVENGE HAD STOMACH FOR THEM ALL.

ALAS, HE IS BETRAYED, AND I UNDONE.

OUT, STRUMPET! WEEP'ST THOU FOR HIM TO MY FACE?

O BANISH ME, MY LORD, BUT KILL ME NOT!

DOWN, STRUMPET!

KILL ME TOMORROW— LET ME LIVE TONIGHT!

NAY, IF YOU STRIVE—

BUT HALF AN HOUR!

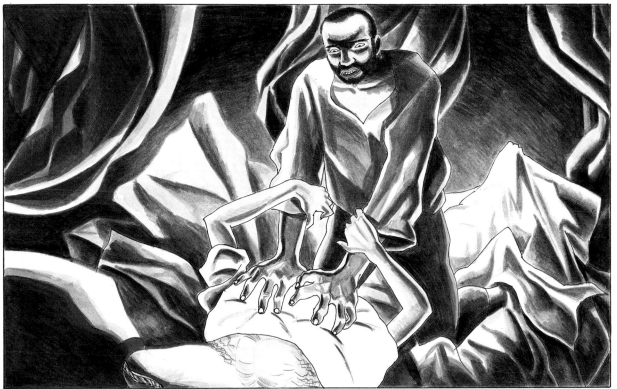

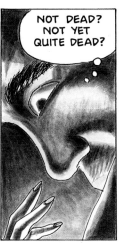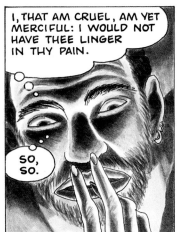

IT IS THE VERY ERROR OF THE MOON; SHE COMES MORE NEARER EARTH THAN SHE WAS WONT, AND MAKES MEN MAD.

CASSIO, MY LORD, HATH KILLED A YOUNG VENETIAN CALLED RODERIGO.

RODERIGO KILLED? AND CASSIO KILLED?

NO, CASSIO IS NOT KILLED.

NOT CASSIO KILLED!

THEN MURDER'S OUT OF TUNE, AND SWEET REVENGE GROWS HARSH.

O, FALSELY, FALSELY MURDERED!

O LORD! WHAT CRY IS THAT?

THAT? WHAT?

OUT AND ALAS, THAT WAS MY LADY'S VOICE!

HELP, HELP, HO, HELP! O, LADY, SPEAK AGAIN!

SWEET DESDEMONA, O SWEET MISTRESS, SPEAK!

A GUILTLESS DEATH I DIE.

O, WHO HATH DONE THIS DEED?

NOBODY—I MYSELF— FAREWELL... COMMEND ME TO MY KIND LORD.

O, FAREWELL!

WHY, HOW SHOULD SHE BE MURDERED?

ALAS, WHO KNOWS?

YOU HEARD HER SAY HERSELF IT WAS NOT I.

SHE SAID SO: I MUST NEEDS REPORT THE TRUTH.

SHE'S LIKE A LIAR GONE TO BURNING HELL: 'TWAS I THAT KILLED HER.

O, THE MORE ANGEL SHE, AND YOU THE BLACKER DEVIL!

SHE TURNED TO FOLLY; AND SHE WAS A WHORE.

THOU DOST BELIE HER, AND THOU ART A DEVIL.

SHE WAS FALSE AS WATER.

THOU ART RASH AS FIRE TO SAY THAT SHE WAS FALSE. O, SHE WAS HEAVENLY TRUE!

119

CASSIO DID TOP HER: ASK THY HUSBAND ELSE. O, I WERE DAMNED BENEATH ALL DEPTH IN HELL BUT THAT I DID PROCEED UPON JUST GROUNDS TO THIS EXTREMITY.

THY HUSBAND KNEW IT ALL.

MY HUSBAND?

THY HUSBAND.

THAT SHE WAS FALSE TO WEDLOCK?

AY, WITH CASSIO.

HAD SHE BEEN TRUE, IF HEAVEN WOULD MAKE ME SUCH ANOTHER WORLD OF ONE ENTIRE AND PERFECT CHRYSOLITE, I'D NOT HAVE SOLD HER FOR IT.

MY HUSBAND?

AY, 'TWAS HE THAT TOLD ME ON HER FIRST: AN HONEST MAN HE IS, AND HATES THE SLIME THAT STICKS ON FILTHY DEEDS.

MY HUSBAND!

WHAT NEEDS THIS ITERANCE, WOMAN? I SAY THY HUSBAND.

O MISTRESS, VILLAINY HATH MADE MOCKS WITH LOVE!

MY HUSBAND SAY THAT SHE WAS FALSE?

HE, WOMAN, — I SAY THY HUSBAND; DOST UNDERSTAND THE WORD? MY FRIEND, THY HUSBAND —HONEST, HONEST, IAGO!

IF HE SAY SO, MAY HIS PERNICIOUS SOUL ROT HALF A GRAIN A DAY!

HE LIES TO TH'HEART.

SHE WAS TOO FOND OF HER MOST FILTHY BARGAIN.

HAH?

DO THY WORST: THIS DEED OF THINE IS NO MORE WORTHY HEAVEN THAN THOU WAST WORTHY HER.

PEACE, YOU WERE BEST.

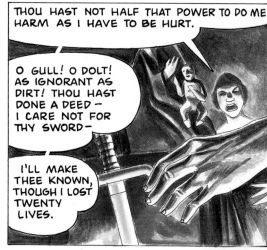

THOU HAST NOT HALF THAT POWER TO DO ME HARM AS I HAVE TO BE HURT.

O GULL! O DOLT! AS IGNORANT AS DIRT! THOU HAST DONE A DEED — I CARE NOT FOR THY SWORD—

I'LL MAKE THEE KNOWN, THOUGH I LOST TWENTY LIVES.

HELP! HELP HO! HELP!

THE MOOR HATH KILLED MY MISTRESS! MURDER! MURDER!

WHAT IS THE MATTER? HOW NOW, GENERAL?

120

O, ARE YOU COME, IAGO? YOU HAVE DONE WELL, THAT MEN MUST LAY THEIR MURDERS ON YOUR NECK.

WHAT IS THE MATTER?

DISPROVE THIS VILLAIN, IF THOU BE'ST A MAN: HE SAID THOU TOLD'ST HIM THAT HIS WIFE WAS FALSE. I KNOW THOU DIDST NOT: THOU'RT NOT SUCH A VILLAIN.

SPEAK, FOR MY HEART IS FULL.

I TOLD HIM WHAT I THOUGHT, AND TOLD NO MORE THAN WHAT HE FOUND HIMSELF WAS APT AND TRUE.

BUT DID YOU EVER TELL HIM SHE WAS FALSE?

I DID.

YOU TOLD A LIE, AN ODIOUS DAMNÈD LIE: UPON MY SOUL, A LIE, A WICKED LIE! SHE, FALSE WITH CASSIO?

DID YOU SAY WITH CASSIO?

WITH CASSIO, MISTRESS! GO TO, CHARM YOUR TONGUE.

I WILL NOT CHARM MY TONGUE; I AM BOUND TO SPEAK: MY MISTRESS HERE LIES MURDERED IN HER BED.

O HEAVENS FORFEND!

AND YOUR REPORTS HAVE SET THE MURDER ON.

NAY, STARE NOT MASTERS: IT IS TRUE INDEED.

'TIS A STRANGE TRUTH.

O MONSTROUS ACT!

VILLAINY, VILLAINY, VILLAINY!

I THINK UPON'T, I THINK— I SMELL'T— O VILLAINY!

I THOUGHT SO THEN; I'LL KILL MYSELF FOR GRIEF.

O VILLAINY, VILLAINY!

WHAT, ARE YOU MAD? I CHARGE YOU GET YOU HOME.

GOOD GENTLEMEN, LET ME HAVE LEAVE TO SPEAK. 'TIS PROPER I OBEY HIM, BUT NOT NOW.

PERCHANCE, IAGO, I WILL NE'ER GO HOME.

O! O! O!

NAY, LAY THEE DOWN AND ROAR, FOR THOU HAST KILLED THE SWEETEST INNOCENT THAT E'ER DID LIFT UP EYE.

O, SHE WAS FOUL!

I SCARCE DID KNOW YOU, UNCLE; THERE LIES YOUR NIECE, WHOSE BREATH INDEED THESE HANDS HAVE NEWLY STOPPED.

I KNOW THIS ACT SHOWS HORRIBLE AND GRIM.

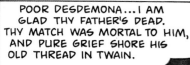

POOR DESDEMONA...I AM GLAD THY FATHER'S DEAD. THY MATCH WAS MORTAL TO HIM, AND PURE GRIEF SHORE HIS OLD THREAD IN TWAIN.

DID HE LIVE NOW, THIS SIGHT WOULD MAKE HIM DO A DESPERATE TURN, YEA, CURSE HIS BETTER ANGEL FROM HIS SIDE, AND FALL TO REPROBANCE.

'TIS PITIFUL: BUT YET IAGO KNOWS THAT SHE WITH CASSIO HATH THE ACT OF SHAME A THOUSAND TIMES COMMITTED.

CASSIO CONFESSED IT, AND SHE DID GRATIFY HIS AMOROUS WORKS WITH THAT RECOGNIZANCE AND PLEDGE OF LOVE WHICH I FIRST GAVE HER.

I SAW IT IN HIS HAND: IT WAS A HANDKERCHIEF, AN ANTIQUE TOKEN MY FATHER GAVE MY MOTHER.

O GOD! O HEAVENLY POWERS!

ZOUNDS, HOLD YOUR PEACE!

'TWILL OUT, 'TWILL OUT. I, PEACE? — NO, I WILL SPEAK AS LIBERAL AS THE NORTH; LET HEAVEN, AND MEN, AND DEVILS, LET THEM ALL, ALL, ALL CRY SHAME AGAINST ME, YET I'LL SPEAK.

BE WISE, AND GET YOU HOME.

I WILL NOT.

FIE! YOUR SWORD UPON A WOMAN?

O THOU DULL MOOR, THAT HANDKERCHIEF THOU SPEAK'ST OF I FOUND BY FORTUNE AND DID GIVE MY HUSBAND; FOR OFTEN, WITH A SOLEMN EARNESTNESS —

MORE THAN INDEED BELONGED TO SUCH A TRIFLE— HE BEGGED OF ME TO STEAL IT.

VILLAINOUS WHORE!

SHE GAVE IT CASSIO? NO, ALAS, I FOUND IT, AND DID GIVE'T MY HUSBAND.

FILTH, THOU LIEST!

122

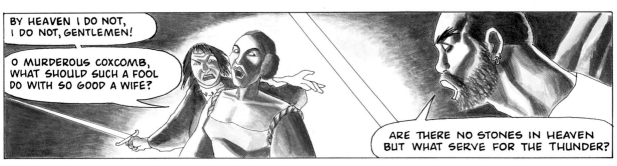

'TIS A NOTORIOUS VILLAIN.— TAKE YOU THIS WEAPON WHICH I HAVE RECOVERED FROM THE MOOR.

COME GUARD THE DOOR WITHOUT: LET HIM NOT PASS, BUT KILL HIM RATHER. I'LL AFTER THAT SAME VILLAIN, FOR 'TIS A DAMNÈD SLAVE.

I AM NOT VALIANT NEITHER, BUT EVERY PUNY WHIPSTER GETS MY SWORD.

BUT WHY SHOULD HONOUR OUTLIVE HONESTY?

LET IT GO —ALL.

WHAT DID THY SONG BODE, LADY?

HARK, CANST THOU HEAR ME? I WILL PLAY THE SWAN AND DIE IN MUSIC.

WILLOW, WILLOW, WILLOW.

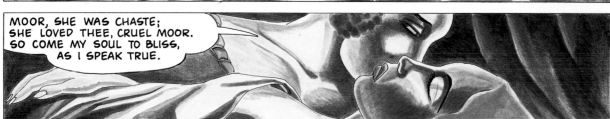

MOOR, SHE WAS CHASTE; SHE LOVED THEE, CRUEL MOOR. SO COME MY SOUL TO BLISS, AS I SPEAK TRUE.

SO, SPEAKING AS I THINK, I DIE, I DIE.

I HAVE ANOTHER WEAPON IN THIS CHAMBER: IT WAS A SWORD OF SPAIN, THE ICE-BROOK'S TEMPER. —O, HERE IT IS.

UNCLE, I MUST COME FORTH!

IF THOU ATTEMPT IT, IT WILL COST THEE DEAR; THOU HAST NO WEAPON, AND PERFORCE MUST SUFFER.

LOOK IN UPON ME THEN, AND SPEAK WITH ME, OR NAKED AS I AM I WILL ASSAULT THEE.

WHAT IS THE MATTER?

BEHOLD, I HAVE A WEAPON!

A BETTER NEVER DID ITSELF SUSTAIN UPON A SOLDIER'S THIGH. I HAVE SEEN THE DAY THAT WITH THIS LITTLE ARM AND THIS GOOD SWORD, I HAVE MADE MY WAY THROUGH MORE IMPEDIMENTS THAN TWENTY TIMES YOUR STOP. BUT, O VAIN BOAST, WHO CAN CONTROL HIS FATE? 'TIS NOT SO NOW.

I LOOK DOWN TOWARDS HIS FEET; BUT THAT'S A FABLE.

IF THAT THOU BE'ST A DEVIL, I CANNOT KILL THEE.

WRENCH HIS SWORD FROM HIM!

I BLEED, SIR, BUT NOT KILLED.

I AM NOT SORRY NEITHER; I'D HAVE THEE LIVE, FOR IN MY SENSE 'TIS HAPPINESS TO DIE.

O THOU OTHELLO, THAT WAST ONCE SO GOOD, FALLEN IN THE PRACTICE OF A DAMNED SLAVE WHAT SHALL BE SAID TO THEE?

WHY, ANYTHING: AN HONOURABLE MURDERER, IF YOU WILL: FOR NAUGHT DID I IN HATE, BUT ALL IN HONOUR.

THIS WRETCH HAS PART CONFESSED HIS VILLAINY. DID YOU AND HE CONSENT IN CASSIO'S DEATH?

AY.

DEAR GENERAL, I NEVER GAVE YOU CAUSE.

I DO BELIEVE IT, AND I ASK YOUR PARDON.

WILL YOU, I PRAY, DEMAND THAT DEMI-DEVIL WHY HE HATH THUS ENSNARED MY SOUL AND BODY?

DEMAND ME NOTHING. WHAT YOU KNOW, YOU KNOW. FROM THIS TIME FORTH I NEVER WILL SPEAK WORD.

WHAT! NOT TO PRAY?

TORMENTS WILL OPE YOUR LIPS.

WELL, THOU DOST BEST.

SIR, YOU SHALL UNDERSTAND WHAT HATH BEFALLEN, WHICH, AS I THINK, YOU KNOW NOT. HERE IS A LETTER FOUND IN THE POCKET OF THE SLAIN RODERIGO, AND HERE ANOTHER.

THE ONE OF THEM IMPORTS THE DEATH OF CASSIO, TO BE UNDERTOOK BY RODERIGO.

O VILLAIN!

MOST HEATHENISH. AND MOST GROSS!

NOW HERE'S ANOTHER DISCONTENTED PAPER FOUND IN HIS POCKET TOO; AND THIS, IT SEEMS, RODERIGO MEANT TO HAVE SENT THIS DAMNED VILLAIN, BUT THAT, BELIKE, IAGO, IN THE NICK CAME IN AND SATISFIED HIM.

O THOU PERNICIOUS CAITIFF!

HOW CAME YOU, CASSIO, BY THAT HANDKERCHIEF THAT WAS MY WIFE'S?

I FOUND IT IN MY CHAMBER; AND HE HIMSELF CONFESSED BUT EVEN NOW THAT THERE HE DROPPED IT FOR A SPECIAL PURPOSE WHICH WROUGHT TO HIS DESIRE.

O FOOL, FOOL, FOOL!

THERE IS BESIDES, IN RODERIGO'S LETTER, HOW HE UPBRAIDS IAGO, THAT HE MADE HIM BRAVE ME UPON THE WATCH, WHEREON IT CAME THAT I WAS CAST.

AND EVEN BUT NOW HE SPAKE, AFTER LONG SEEMING DEAD— IAGO HURT HIM, IAGO SET HIM ON.

YOU MUST FORSAKE THIS ROOM AND GO WITH US. YOUR POWER AND YOUR COMMAND IS TAKEN OFF AND CASSIO RULES IN CYPRUS.

FOR THIS SLAVE, IF THERE BE ANY CUNNING CRUELTY THAT CAN TORMENT HIM MUCH, AND HOLD HIM LONG, IT SHALL BE HIS.

YOU SHALL CLOSE PRISONER REST, TILL THAT THE NATURE OF YOUR FAULT BE KNOWN TO THE VENETIAN STATE.

COME, BRING HIM AWAY.

SOFT YOU; A WORD OR TWO BEFORE YOU GO. I HAVE DONE THE STATE SOME SERVICE, AND THEY KNOW'T: NO MORE OF THAT.

THEN MUST YOU SPEAK OF ONE THAT LOVED NOT WISELY, BUT TOO WELL;

I PRAY YOU IN YOUR LETTERS, WHEN YOU SHALL THESE UNLUCKY DEEDS RELATE, SPEAK OF ME AS I AM: NOTHING EXTENUATE, NOR SET DOWN AUGHT IN MALICE.

OF ONE NOT EASILY JEALOUS BUT, BEING WROUGHT, PERPLEXED IN THE EXTREME; OF ONE WHOSE HAND, LIKE THE BASE INDIAN, THREW A PEARL AWAY RICHER THAN ALL HIS TRIBE; OF ONE WHOSE SUBDUED EYES, ALBEIT UNUSÈD TO THE MELTING MOOD, DROP TEARS AS FAST AS THE ARABIAN TREES THEIR MED'CINABLE GUM...

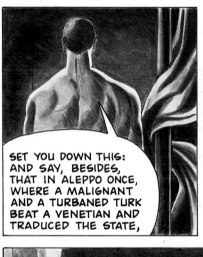

SET YOU DOWN THIS: AND SAY, BESIDES, THAT IN ALEPPO ONCE, WHERE A MALIGNANT AND A TURBANED TURK BEAT A VENETIAN AND TRADUCED THE STATE,

I TOOK BY TH'THROAT THE CIRCUMCISÈD DOG, AND SMOTE HIM— THUS!

O BLOODY PERIOD!

ALL THAT IS SPOKE IS MARRED!

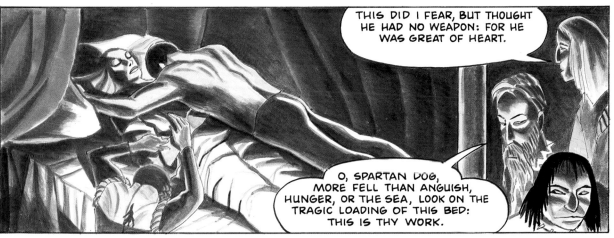